THE JUDGE'S TASK

How Award-Winning Quilts Are Selected

THE JUDGE'S TASK

How Award-Winning Quilts Are Selected

**Patricia J. Morris
Defines Blue Ribbon
Criteria**

Library of Congress Cataloging-in-Publication Data

Morris, Patricia J.
    The judge's task : how award-winning quilts are selected / Patricia J.
    Morris. defines blue ribbon criteria
        p.   cm. –
    ISBN 0-89145-823-9 : $19.95
    1. Quilting–Competitions.   I. Title.
TT835.m688   1993
746.9'7'07973–dc20   93–28509
                                                                    CIP

Additional copies of this book may be ordered from:

American Quilter's Society
P.O. Box 3290
Paducah, KY 42002-3290
@19.95. Add $1.00 for postage and handling.

FOREWORD

Anyone who has ever attended a competitive quilt show has probably come away asking questions about what judges do. What do they look for? What do they see that others do not? Frequently people do not fully understand the awards made in shows, and occasionally judges' decisions are viewed as aberrations, as evidence of bias, or even as sheer lunacy. Why did *this* quilt place and *that* one not?

The answer is not simple and begins with a better understanding of the judge's task. This book has developed because of the American Quilter's Society's belief that such an understanding is important. It is our hope that through greater knowledge of the judge's difficult task, both those who enter and those who attend competitive quilt shows will have a better understanding of what makes an award-winning quilt.

CONTENTS

SECTION ONE:

An Introduction to the Tools and the Process

"I have asked the judges in three large shows what they especially saw in the Sweepstakes quilt. Three different places said exactly these words – 'It was flaw-less.' So, I guess it has to be a combination of 'knock-your-socks-off beauty, and perfection."

HELEN KELLEY

AQS Show Winner

Clearly, the task of the judge or panel of judges is to evaluate all entries submitted into competition and to give recognition to the best of these entries. In evaluating the entries, judges are guided by the rules of the contest – rules established by the show sponsor, and given to all entrants along with the entry form.

These rules may vary in detail and format, but generally they spell out very clearly who is eligible to enter, what types of quilts may be entered, and exactly how and when to enter. The 1994 AQS Quilt Show & Contest entry form and rules are shown as an example in Figures 1a and 1b on pages 11 and 12. The quiltmaker entering a competition must thoroughly understand these rules and abide by them, and so must the judges when they are reviewing the quilts.

The rules and entry forms often involve the determination of an appropriate category for entry. To facilitate the judging process most competitions, especially the larger ones, provide a variety of categories, and entrants must decide into which category their work best fits. The categories are generally, although not always, the obvious ones based on technique, such as Pieced, Appliquéd, Mixed, Special, and so on. These broad categories may be further broken down in Traditional and Innovative,

1994 AQS Quilt Contest Rules

1. Anyone can enter a cloth quilt by submitting slides and entry blank.

2. Quilt must be constructed & quilted by person(s) named on entry blank.

3. All quilt entries are to be made by one person except in the Group Quilt category.

4. All quilts must be quilted either by hand or machine.

5. All quilt entries will be considered for Best of Show, Gingher, Bernina & Best Wall Quilt purchase awards. Winners in these four divisions not wishing to relinquish their quilts may retain possession of their quilts by relinquishing their prize money. Photographing & printing rights must still be granted to AQS.

6. Quilt must have been finished after 1991 and be in excellent condition.

7. Quilts displayed in previous AQS shows are ineligible.

8. Limit two entries per person, one quilt per category. No kits, please.

9. Quilts in categories 1 thru 9 must be at least 60" wide & at least 80" in length or larger.

10. Wall quilts must be minimum size 40" x 40"; maximum size 80" x 80" and not framed with wood, metal, etc.

11. Quilts that are both pieced & appliqued should be entered in the category of the technique which predominates.

12. Other Techniques include whole cloth, trapunto, batik, stenciled, embroidered, etc.

13. Incomplete, torn or soiled quilts will not qualify for entry or exhibition.

14. Quilt must be available for judging and display from April 4 through May 3, 1994.

15. Free entry to AQS members. Non-members must enclose $25.00 with entry blank. Make checks payable to American Quilter's Society.

16. Prize winners will be notified by phone. Awards will be presented at the Awards Banquet, Friday evening, April 22nd, or will be mailed to those unable to attend.

17. Security will be provided.

To Enter Send:
    (a) completed & signed entry blank with correct category circled (incomplete entry blank will be returned)
    (b) 2 slides only (1 full view & 1 close-up)
    (c) a self-addressed, 58¢ stamped business-size envelope
    (d) entry fee (if you are not an AQS member)

Timetable

January 15,1994	Slides, entry blank and SASE must be received by AQS or postmarked, no later than Jan. 15,1994. No slides of quilts accepted for competition will be returned.
March 15, 1994	All entrants will be notified. If your quilt is accepted, instructions will be included on sending your quilt for judging.
April 4, 1994	Accepted quilts must be received by the American Quilter's Society, 5801 Kentucky Dam Road, Paducah, KY 42003.

Figure 1a. *Sample: 1994 AQS Quilt show rules.*

1994 AQS Quilt Contest!!!

Entry Blank To Accompany Slides (may be photocopied)

Membership #_____

Name(s) _____
(Please Print)   List additional names on back of entry form.

Street_____

City _____ State ___ Zip_____

Phone   (_____)_____

Local Newspaper _____

Circle **One** Category Number:
Original Design: Yes ☐   No ☐

Machine Quilted: Yes ☐   No ☐

Quilt Title _____

Quilt Size (inches) _____

Basic Techniques_____

_____

Brief Description of Quilt for Show Booklet_____

_____

_____

_____

_____

Approximate Insurance Value $ _____
(Maximum $5,000.00)

I wish to enter the above item and agree to abide by the rules & decisions of the judges. I understand that AQS will take every precaution to protect my quilt exhibited in this show. I realize they cannot be responsible for the acts of nature beyond their control. You may have my permission to photograph this quilt. If my quilt is exhibited in the American Quilter's Society Show, I understand that my signature gives AQS the right to use a photo of my quilt in any publications, advertisements or promotional materials.

Signature_____

Social Security #_____
Please put your name on the slide mounts & mail slides, entry blank & 58¢ SASE to: **American Quilter's Society,** Klaudeen Hansen, P.O. Box 3290, Dept. Entry, Paducah, KY 42002-3290.

Figure 1b. *Sample: 1994 AQS Quilt show entry form.*

Amateur and Professional, Bed Quilts and Wallhangings, and as many other divisions as imaginative show sponsors can devise. This grouping of the entries into categories allows the judges to deal with one relatively homogenous portion of the quilts at a time, which makes evaluation a more manageable process.

When judging a quilt show with categories, the judges look at one category at a time, reviewing each entry for its overall impact and its detail. The best quilts in each category are chosen and the awards are made. The awards for a given category are usually first, second, and third place along with one or two honorable mentions. Once one category is completed, the judges move on to the next and repeat the process of choosing the best.

When all of the categories have been judged, the judges look at the first place winner in each. It is from among these blue ribbon winners that the Best of Show is chosen. After the Best of Show is named, any other special awards peculiar to that competition are chosen. These special awards, usually specified in the contest rules, can be awards such as Best First Quilt, Best Workmanship, Best Design, or Best Color Use.

Because all of the awards given often grow out of the initial category judging, it is

"Entering competitions gives you the opportunity to see where your skills can be improved and also the opportunity to share your work with other quilters."

JANICE R. STREETER
AQS Show Winner

"Competitions are excellent,
but their value and effect
depend on where you are
with your work, and why
you are entering."

SARA ANN MCLENNAND
AQS Show Winner

very important that each quilt be entered by its maker in the correct category as defined by the sponsoring organization. A quilt entered into an inappropriate category may be disqualified by the judges if it does not meet certain criteria such as a minimum dimension, and in cases where it is not totally disqualified, it will most certainly not do well in competition. If selecting the best category for a particular quilt is difficult, the maker is encouraged to contact the show sponsor for assistance.

In addition to determining the rules of the competition and setting up the categories, the show sponsors also select the judges and decide on the method of judging that will be used. Often either a point system or an elimination system is developed, and the judges use this method as the framework within which their decisions are made.

If a point system is used, various numbers of points are assigned to each area of the quilt being evaluated. If the total possible points for a quilt is 100, then specific numbers of points are assigned, such as twelve points for color use and eight points for the quilting stitch (Figure 2).

When looking at a quilt, the judge determines whether the color use should receive only one point, all twelve points, or some number in between. The number is

ENTRY # _____

Judges Score Sheet   Score

General Appearance *(10 points)* ...._____

Design *(30 points)* ...._____

Color *(10 points)* ...._____

Top Construction *(30 points)* ...._____

Quilting *(10 points)* ...._____

Finishing *(10 points)* ...._____

                                    _____

TOTAL POINTS ...._____

Figure 2. *Sample: score sheet.*

American Quilter's Society   Entry # _____
P.O. Box 3290
Paducah, KY 42002-3290   Award _____

Judges' Comment Sheet

Title _____

Best features of this quilt are:

Areas that need improvement are:

Judged by:

(The comments made about your quilt are
not intended to serve as an in-depth critique.)

Thank you for sharing your quilt, making this another great show!

Figure 3. *Sample: AQS Judge's comment sheet.*

recorded on the form, and then the same approach is used for determining how many of the eight possible points for quilting stitch should be awarded, and how many points should be assigned for each of the other quilt areas. The points on the score sheet are then added up and the quilt with the highest number of points becomes the first place winner, the quilt with the next highest number of points becomes the second place winner, and so on down the set of awards for that category.

The great disadvantage of the point system is that assigning a certain number of points, say eight out of a possible ten points for a specific detail, does not convey much helpful information when the score sheet is returned to the maker. This can be remedied by an area on the evaluation form reserved for comments, but frequently only numbers are assigned by the judges.

Perhaps the greatest potential weakness of the point system of rating a quilt is that if an area appears on the score sheet but not on the entry being evaluated the entire scoring of that entry becomes problematic, if not invalid. A quilt with no borders, for example, would be able to receive no points in the area of borders.

When an elimination system is used, a form such as the one shown at left in Figure 3 can be used. All the quilts in the category

"Get a 'feel' for the contest before you attempt to enter a work. Also be very careful that for the jurying you submit clear, sharp slides that do justice to your work. Take as many as 10 different snapshots of the quilt with 10 different settings and use the best ones."

ARNOLD H. SAVAGE
AQS Show Winner

17

are looked at and comments are made on each entry. The American Quilters Society judges currently use this system of evaluation in determining the award winners for their quilt show & contest.

Quilts with weaknesses that would prevent them from winning an award are removed and the remaining quilts are looked at again. Once more the weaker quilts are removed. When only the very best quilts remain, the judges assign awards to specific quilts. This final determination is based to a great extent on the comments that were made by judges during the detailed review of each entry, when it was noted how well these contending entries measured up against each other.

While judges and show sponsors each have preferred judging methods, the great advantage of the elimination system of judging is that the judges are guided by what appears in the quilt being reviewed, not by an arbitrary list on a score sheet which may, or may not, be appropriate for the piece being evaluated. In addition, when this system is used, the specific feedback on the comment sheet conveys useful information to the maker.

"When you enter your work in competition, follow all rules of the competition carefully and be willing to accept the judges' decisions graciously, even though you personally may not agree."

ANNABEL BAUGHER
AQS Show Winner

SECTION TWO:

JUDGING QUILTS

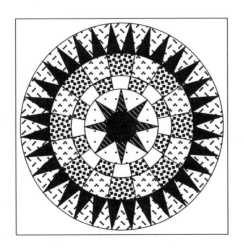

Once the judges are on site and the judging begins, each quilt is evaluated by means of as thorough a review as possible of all of the quilt's various aspects. Generally speaking, there are three broad areas in which the judges evaluate details: design, workmanship, and general appearance. These aspects of a quilt cannot be literally separated from each other, but judges can separate them for the purposes of discussion. Most often, in evaluating these areas, equal weight is given to design and workmanship, and the area of general appearance is given less weight than those areas.

DESIGN

The area of design is comprised of all the visual, aesthetic aspects of the piece, as opposed to the technical or mechanical aspects. When the area of quilt design is being evaluated, design can be further broken down into two parts: the design of the quilt top and the design of the quilting.

In evaluating the design of the quilt top, the judge looks at the way in which the pattern elements do or do not unite and whether they are all in proportion to each other and to the overall size of the piece. Is there a good relationship between the design motif and the background? It is likely that in a pieced work the "background" is actually what is just seen as background

"I feel proud when something I enjoy doing measures up in competition, and it pleases me to know others have enjoyed seeing my quilts in shows."

MARCIA J. LUTZ
AQS Show Winner

because of the use of fabrics; in an appliquéd work, one is often looking at the relationship between what is figure and what is literally a physical background. Regardless, the figure and background areas should have proper proportions. The figure should not be so small it looks lost in a sea of background, as it does in Figure 4. The proportions of these two elements should be visually pleasing, and show the figure to its best advantage.

Each entry should be a single entity with well integrated parts. Secondary

"Always strive for accuracy and neatness in all steps of quiltmaking. If you have accomplished these essential requirements and skill, feel confident in entering your quilt in competition."

DOROTHY ARENDT
AQS Show Winner

FIG. 4. Appliqué block with a much too small motif for the size of background area.

"I realized a long time ago when going to quilt shows how much I appreciated others for entering their quilts so I could enjoy them. It only seemed right to pay back by entering my quilts as soon as they were presentable."

DOREEN SPECKMANN
AQS Show Winner

design motifs that "merge" with primary design areas are looked at by judges to make certain they don't detract from the primary design. Rather, these secondary designs should add interest and enhance the primary design.

It is important that no individual detail draw so much attention to itself that focus is stolen from the piece as a unified presentation. These details, though, must have some character. There must be enough of interest in the individual elements to prevent the piece from becoming static.

The different sections of a quilt top should also integrate well and become a unified whole. For instance, the primary units of the piece should relate to the block set, whether the set is block to block, alternate plain block, sashed, or another less usual arrangement. The entire center area of the quilt should relate well to the border and to the edge finishing. The entry should not look as if it were composed of parts of many very different quilts.

The textures used to highlight and make the top design more visually interesting should do just that. They shouldn't muddy or obscure the design or cancel out the linear qualities of the piece. Texture appeals to the sense of touch, even when the item cannot be physically touched. Texture is created by the various fabrics used, their

22

properties, and their relationships to each other. The patterns of the fabrics employed add significantly to the texture of the quilt or wallhanging. The fabrics chosen should enhance the design and be suitable to each other and to the design.

QUILT TOP

The design of a quilt top should be balanced. There should be an even-handed, equal distribution of visual weight. The design should be interesting, but looking at the entry, the viewer shouldn't be visually pulled off balance by the design.

Unity is also a necessary component of a successful design, but variety and contrast must also be present to avoid monotony. The successful design will elicit a response of some kind from the viewer, whether that response is positive or negative; the work will not simply be a "walkpast" quilt. The judge's job, though, is to by-pass or go beyond any such initial response to carefully review the quilt on the basis of its various merits.

One of the most important factors in evaluating the design of entries in a quilt competition is color. Most viewers of quilts react first to the use of color. Color is important for the judge, too, and its use is reviewed carefully to determine whether it is handled to best advantage in each quilt.

"The one thing I urge quilters to do is enter shows. That is the most effective way to compare your work to others."

KATHERINE E. INMAN
AQS Show Winner

"Make something that you are really interested in and enthusiastic about. Whether you think you will enter it in competition or not, make it because you like it. Then enter if you want. Just entering is good; winning is great."

LUCY BURTSCHI GRADY
AQS Show Winner

The use of individual colors is considered, as is the relationships among the colors. Does the use of color highlight and emphasize the design or does it work against it. There are no right colors or wrong colors for a given design. Rather, success is a matter of how well the colors used work together and with the design.

When the quilt incorporates a traditional design, the judges look at how well the traditional pattern is interpreted through the use of today's fabrics and the maker's personal approach to color. And, as with non-traditional work, a traditional quilt is looked at to see whether it is a completely realized entity that effectively communicates through its components of design, color, and fabric use.

QUILTING

In addition to evaluating the design of a quilt's constructed top, the judges also rate the design of the quilting, the pattern of quilting stitches, including the background support quilting. The quilting design should complement the quilt top design, not interfere with or work against it. This quilting design should work with the top design to produce an integrated piece.

The quilting design should fit well into all the areas of the quilt, having been enlarged, reduced, or modified as needed

(Figure 5a and 5b). This is especially important for problem areas such as sashings and borders, and corners where the borders turn. In these areas a design will very often need to be reduced, enlarged, or modified to work well.

In summation, the quilting design should emphasize the elements of the top design and be in proportion to the pattern design and the overall size of the entry, while at the same time being technically suitable for the filler used.

The amount of quilting should be balanced over the entire quilt; this is very important to the visual impact of the work. It is also important technically as a quilt with an imbalance in the amount of quilting will

FIG. 5a. *A quilting design that is too small for its area.*

FIG. 5b. *Design 5a modified to fill the area better.*

25

seldom "square up" (have straight sides and ninety-degree angle corners). Nor is it likely to lie or hang flat.

The placement, type, and amount of background support quilting can contribute immeasurably to the overall effectiveness of the piece. It can provide a backdrop against which the other portions of the quilting design and the various top elements are displayed to best advantage. Effective background quilting makes the entire piece look planned and complete.

If the background quilting takes the form of a grid, the grid should be positioned so its segments touch adjoining edges at the same point and angle (Figures 6a and 6b). If the grid is not carefully placed on the top,

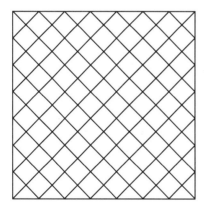

FIG. 6a. *Well laid out grid of back-ground support quilting.*

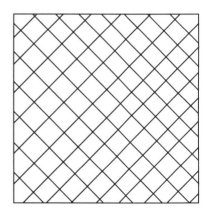

FIG. 6b. *Poorly laid out grid of background support quilting. Grid meets at varying angles. Note variation in triangles along the top.*

the design of the entire quilt or wallhanging can look out of whack, which will definitely affect the response of the viewer. A grid must be satisfactorily resolved technically in order for it to influence the visual aspect of the work positively.

Just as the fabric colors and their relationships can affect the success of a quilt design, so can the quilting thread colors. Traditionally, white and off-white quilting threads were always safe choices. They remain safe choices, though not always necessarily the best or most imaginative. Whatever color quilting thread is used, whether white, off-white, or any other imaginable color or combination of colors, the color(s) should enhance the entry while not distracting from the quilt top design.

A judge reviewing a quilt will be concerned that the quilting thread color works with all of the other elements and that it isn't causing a visual problem. If metallic thread is used for quilting, it should add to the effectiveness of the piece and should not draw undue attention to itself at the expense of the unity and integrity of the work. In addition to any special effects which may be created by the use of metallic thread, the colors of such threads are considered in the same way as any other quilting thread color.

In every way the quilting design should

"Enjoy your quiltmaking first and always. Sharing in a competition is an added pleasure. It is helpful for you to see your work in an impersonal setting. Take the judges' comments and go forward from there."

MARTHA B. SKELTON

AQS Show Winner

complement the overall top design, integrating with it and adding interest.

It is important to keep in mind that no single aspect of the design of a quilt will make or break its chances for receiving an award. The judges are looking at the overall success of the design – how well the elements are united and integrated and how successful the piece is as a whole.

WORKMANSHIP

Rating workmanship involves an inspection of all the technical, mechanical elements of the fabric work. First the judges consider the technique(s) employed to realize the design. The technique(s) chosen for rendering a given design should be suitable to that design, and the entire top should be flat and even, without distortions caused by technique. The two techniques most often seen, used either alone or in combination, are piecing and appliqué.

PIECED ENTRIES

In evaluating pieced entries, the judges look to see that all of the blocks, if indeed, the top is made up of blocks, are uniform in size. An unevenness in block size can throw the entire top out of alignment. The pieces composing the top should be accurately cut and consistently placed in relation to the grain of the fabric. This means that

"It adds validity to one's work when it is well received in major competition, and tends to make you challenge yourself to do as well with the next piece."

EILEEN BAHRING

SULLIVAN

AQS Show Winner

the grain should be logically and/or imaginatively exploited (Figure 7).

All of the corners and points in the design, whether they involve four-point meets or forty-point meets, should be exact (Figures 8a and 8b, page 30). If the pieced pattern used has curved seams, these seams should be smoothly curved without any flatted-out areas (Figures 9a and 9b, page 30).

The color of the thread used to piece the units should match or blend with the fabrics. The seam allowances should be carefully handled, pressed consistently to one side or the other (or even open if the chosen pattern requires this). Where neces-

"Competition is tough. It can never seem 'fair' to everyone, but it's a fantastic motivator."

JOY BAAKLINI
AQS Show Winner

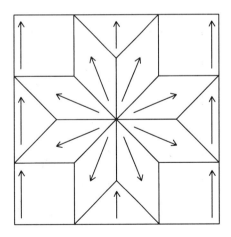

FIG. 7. *Grain should be used logically.*

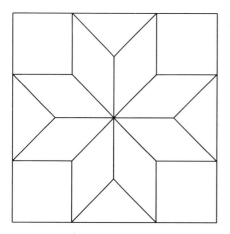

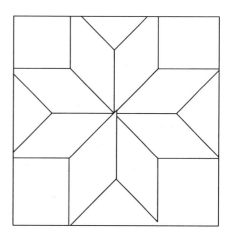

FIG. 8a. *Good meeting of eight points at center and outer edges of block.*

FIG. 8b. *Poor meeting of eight points at center and outer edges of block.*

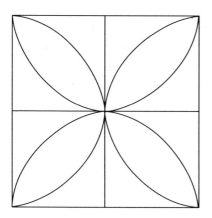

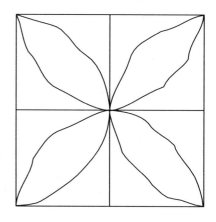

FIG. 9a. *Smoothly curved pieced seams.*

FIG. 9b. *Poorly handled curved pieced seams.*

sary, seams should be trimmed to reduce bulk. Also, seam allowances should be graded wherever there is a possibility of their shadowing through the top fabric. The pencil lines used as cutting or stitching guidelines should not be allowed to shadow through the top either.

The fabrics used in the entry should be compatible with each other and with the quilt's intended use. Fabrics that can be successfully combined in a wall piece may not be entirely suitable combined in a utility bed quilt.

There are several types of fabrics that should always be used very carefully. A significant problem frequently surfaces when regularly patterned fabrics are used. Stripes, dots, and other more subtle patterns should be carefully cut in relation to the pattern of the fabric. If the fabric has not been printed straight on the yardage, that may mean you need to cut slightly off grain. If the fabric isn't cut straight with the pattern, a cockeyed look which is disturbing to the eye may result. This problem becomes more severe the larger the cut piece of patterned fabric.

When used off-whack in the border, these fabric pieces can cause real problems for the viewer (Figure 10, page 32). Of course, it is a different matter if striped fabrics are being purposefully used in a

"Don't take rejection of your quilt as rejection of yourself. Keep entering other competitions. Other judges may judge it differently. Keep trying!"

KAREN MAGUIRE
AQS Show Winner

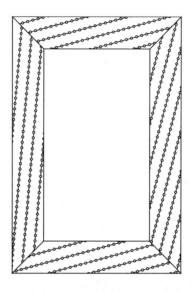

FIG. 10. *Regularly patterned fabric poorly handled in border area.*

FIG. 11. *Darker fabrics shadowing through in an appliqué block: stem end and leaf ends under flower and flower under center of blossom.*

cockeyed manner to further a special intended effect of the work. However, it is very important that such an unusual use clearly further the effect of the work or the quiltmaker will run the risk of being penalized for using these special fabrics poorly.

All the stitching on a pieced work should be strong, tight, and not visible, whether done by machine or by hand. All of the loose threads and frays on the reverse side of the quilt top should be trimmed off and should not show through the quilt top. As to whether the work should be pieced by hand or machine, that is the maker's choice. The judges are not influenced by which method has been used (as long as it meets the requirements of the competition).

APPLIQUÉD ENTRIES

In evaluating appliquéd entries, judges check the uniformity of block size if the top is composed of such units. Most judges feel that the grain of all the background blocks should run in the same direction, preferably vertically. The appliqué motifs should have the grain used to best advantage.

There should be no raw edges on any of the appliqué pieces, and all of the basting stitches should have been removed. There should be no shadowing through of either darker color appliqué motifs (Figure 11) or of a darker color background beneath

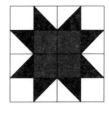

"Enter competitions. But, take the outcome of competition with grace, whether you win or lose. A single quilt is a fraction of our worth."

DEBRA WAGNER
AQS Show Winner

lighter color appliqué motifs.

The judges also check the curves of the appliqué pieces. All of the inside and outside curves should be smoothly executed (Figures 12a and 12b). By the same token, both the inside and outside points should be truly pointed (Figures 13a and 13b).

The shapes of the individual appliqué pieces should be uniformly maintained. For instance, if a flower is meant to have four uniform petals and three uniform leaves, all four petals should be of the same size and shape, as should the three leaves. If the same appliqué motif appears in block after block, it should be consistently positioned in each of the blocks.

"I often wonder if I would make as many quilts if I didn't enter them in shows. Judged shows are a very important part of quilting."

LINDA CANTRELL
AQS Show Winner

Judges keep various possibilities in mind when checking the stitching method used to attach the appliqué pieces to the background. Some quiltmakers use hidden stitches, which should not be obvious. Other quiltmakers use visible attaching and/or decorative stitches, which should enhance the design. Whatever type of stitches are used – hidden, blind, running, ladder, blanket, embroidery, etc. – they should be uniformly done, small, tight, and as close together as the stitch type requires. The primary purpose of appliqué stitches is to keep the appliqué units firmly attached to the background and they should accomplish this.

FIG. 12a. *Appliqué with inside and outside curves smoothly curved.*

FIG. 12b. *Appliqué with inside and ouside curves poorly handled.*

FIG. 13a. *Appliqué with inside and outside points truly sharp.*

FIG. 13b. *Appliqué with outside point blunted and inside point curved and distorted.*

"I believe that quiltmakers should always make the quilts that come from the heart, the ones they most want to make. I don't think that any quiltmaker ought to compromise designs or ideas just to fit the rules of a particular contest."

CARYL BRYER FALLERT

AQS Show Winner

As to the choice of thread color for appliqué stitching, it should not be visible if an unobtrusive stitching method is used.. If a visible or decorative stitching method is used, the thread color may either match or contrast with the color of the piece being applied, but the thread color shouldn't call undue attention to itself, stealing focus from the appliqué design.

If machine satin stitch appliqué is the technique being evaluated, the judges check how well the machine stitching was handled on the curved areas (both inside and outside curves) and in the point areas (both inside and outside points). The stitches should be smoothly laid, even, should cover the edges completely, be consistently at the same angle to the motif, and should have no lumpy, overstitched portions (Figure 14).

The thread color used for this type of machine appliqué should not overwhelm the appliqué pieces. If a machine blind stitch is being reviewed by judges, the secure attachment of the pieces is checked, as is the "invisibility" of the stitches. For other types of machine appliqué, the appropriate criteria are applied. Above all, regardless of the appliqué method used, the pieces should be firmly attached without the type of stitch or the thread color detracting from the work.

OTHER TECHNIQUES

Beyond the use of piecing or appliqué in the construction of the quilt top, or the combination of these two, there are many other top techniques that are employed. Judges see them all from time to time. Whether the technique is embroidery, shadow appliqué, stained glass, Hawaiian-style, or any of a myriad of others, the judges evaluate them in the same way: on the effectiveness of the design, the use of color, the general appearance of the work and the workmanship.

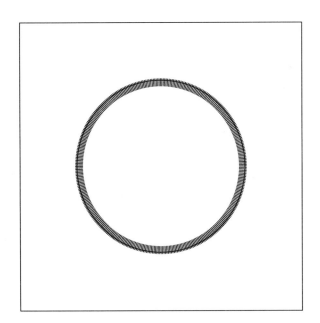

FIG. 14. *Machine satin stitch smoothly covering edges of appliqué motif.*

"*Being a housewife doesn't get rave reviews (even as important as I consider it to be) but produce an award-winning quilt and people seem to sit up and take notice.*"

JUNE CULVEY
AQS Show Winner

Judges look for the use of the proper technique and appropriate materials, and for good handling of the technique. Each special type of quilt must be looked at in its own way – a way based on the special characteristics of its type.

SET OF THE QUILT

In addition to the major techniques used in the construction of the quilt top, the judges also investigate the set of the quilt. The set is how the elements (usually

"Neatness is the most important thing in quiltmaking. It shows proper respect for the materials one uses."

RUMI O'BRIEN
AQS Show Winner

FIG. 15. *Blocks set side by side.*

blocks) are joined to make up the entire quilt top. The three most usual sets that judges see are blocks joined side by side, blocks joined using alternate plain blocks, and blocks joined by sashing.

When looking at a quilt that has the blocks joined side by side or solid (Figure 15), the judges check the block meets – the areas where block edges come together. Where the overall design is dependent on interlocking blocks, these meets are crucial (Figure 16). Wherever there are corners or

FIG. 16. *It is crucial that blocks meet accurately.*

"*Competitions give us personally an opportunity to grow and offer new inspirations and ideas to those who come to see the work.*"

JUDY ANNE WALTER
AQS Show Winner

points, they should meet precisely, and all seam allowances should be properly handled. The thread color should not be obtrusive and the stitching should be strong.

When looking at a quilt that has blocks joined using alternate plain blocks (Figure 17), the grain should be consistent in the alternate plain blocks. As with the side by side set, the corners and points should all meet precisely and all seam allowances should be correctly handled. The thread color should not be obtrusive and the stitch-

"*Winning always produces a shot of much needed self-esteem.*"

JUNE CULVEY
AQS Show Winner

FIG. 17. *Blocks set with alternate plain blocks.*

ing should be strong.

When judges evaluate quilts set with sashing (Figure 18), they check to see that the sashing strips are consistent in size and of a width appropriate to the blocks and the other top elements. There should be no rippling (gathering, bunching, pleating) of the sashing or the block edge where the two join. Judges view the sashing to be sure it is completely straight, down and across the quilt or diagonally from corner to corner, depending on whether the blocks are set

FIG. 18. *Blocks set with sashing, using posts where sashing intersects.*

"As a quilt judge certified by the NQA, I see a continual improvement in our quilt-making. Much of this improvement, I think, is because many of our shows are judged shows."

BONNIE K. BROWNING
AQS Show Winner

on the square or on point.

Over the years, judges have learned that this detail is one that is often a problem – frequently the sashings wobble (Figure 19), i.e., they waver to one side and then to the other, rather than running straight. Sashings that wobble can greatly detract from the success of the individual blocks. Just as in the other sets discussed, the corners and points should all meet precisely and all seam allowances should be carefully handled. The thread color should not be obtrusive and the stitching should be strong.

"In order to complete quilts, you have to set priorities.... having a competition deadline helps."

TERESA TUCKER YOUNG
AQS Show Winner

FIG. 19. *Blocks set with sashing that wobbles.*

BORDERS

The borders of a quilt are yet another important component of the work. Judges check the width of the border, which should be compatible in size with all of the elements of the central area. The width of the borders on all sides should be consistent with each other, or, if not consistent, at least logical in the manner in which they differ. Grain of the border pieces should have been used to best advantage and directional placement should not distract from the work. The border corners may be mitered, squared (straight across/down), set in, or curved (Figures 20a through 20e, pages 44-45), as long as the technique chosen is appropriate to the rest of the piece and the workmanship is precise.

The borders should be of a "oneness" with the central area, serving to emphasize the major elements of the quilt top and at the same time focus the viewer's attention on that area. This is especially important for traditional work.

In non-traditional work, the borders should likewise enhance the central design but the design may also be allowed to extend into the border itself, and sometimes the border may intrude into the main body of the work. However, the border of a quilt, traditional or non-traditional, should not appear to stand alone or apart from the

"Each judge and each contest is different. Not winning is disheartening but not the end of the world – because there's always another show, and another chance."

MARLA HATTABAUGH
AQS Show Winner

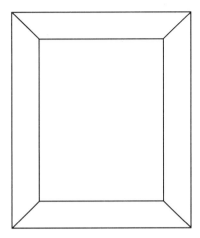

FIG. 20a. *Border corners that are mitered.*

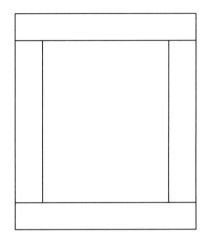

FIG. 20b. *Border corners that are squared across.*

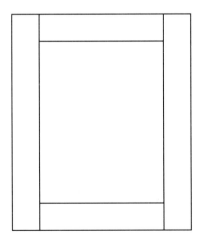

FIG. 20c. *Border corners that are squared down.*

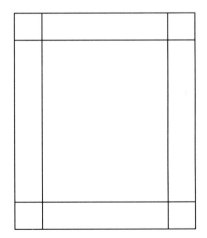

FIG. 20d. *Border corners that are set in.*

body of the quilt work.

The borders should be smoothly attached without rippling (gathering, bunching, pleating). They should be straight without any wobbles either technically (caused by the stitching or other factors) or visually (caused by less than careful use of regularly patterned fabric). The seam allowances on the borders should be properly handled and all meets should be exact. The thread color should not be obtrusive and the stitching should be strong.

In addition to judging quilts with borders, judges also see quilts that have no borders. There are quilts that do not need borders. So as long as the entry is successful without a border, judges will not insist

"Try to be as accurate as possible with every phase of your quilt. If it doesn't look right, take it out and start over."

MARY RUSHING
AQS Show Winner

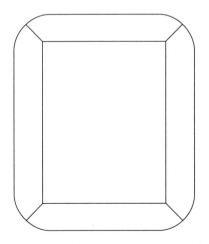

FIG. 20e. *Border "corners" that are curved.*

that it have one. Judges are there to evaluate what is placed before them, rather than to judge what is not there or to redesign, recolor, or re-sew the piece.

QUILTING

The one technique that the judges are called upon to evaluate perhaps more than any other is the quilting. Generally speaking, whether the entry is pieced, appliquéd, or constructed using a combination of these or any other top technique, in most competitions quilting is required in order for a piece to be eligible, so the judges will review the quilting.

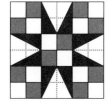

"Begin the project and stay with it until it is finished. That's the only thing accepted in competition: a finished product."

AUDREE L. SELLS
AQS Show Winner

Front (Top) of Quilt

Back (Bottom) of Quilt

FIG. 21. *Quilting stitches and the spaces between them should be even.*

46

The stitches are examined closely. The quilting stitches and the spaces between them should be even on the front and back of the piece (Figure 21), and they should be uniform in size. In general the size of the stitches should be small, but the smallness of the size will be governed by the overall materials used in the work and the thickness of the textile sandwich. Judges will not unrealistically demand incredibly tiny quilting stitches if the physical characteristics of the work do not allow for them or if the design does not support them. The number of quilting stitches per inch (and this is a count that judges rarely make) should be compatible with the fabric, the filler, the design, and the complexity of the seams and not some arbitrarily imposed "ideal" number of stitches.

Any straight quilting lines should be straight and the individual stitches themselves should be straight without slanting (Figures 22a and 22b, page 48). Any curved quilting lines should be smoothly curved. If there are parallel lines of quilting, they should be uniformly parallel (Figures 23a and 23b, page 48). throughout the piece and without any "herringbone-type pulling" between the lines (Figure 24, page 49).

One of the most often seen problems with quilting results from the marking of lines. These lines should not be visible

"Don't make quilts for particular shows – just make the pieces that you really want to make. There are enough shows out there for you to choose one that's right for you."

LINDA MACDONALD
AQS Show Winner

FIG. 22a. *Quilting stitches should be straight.*

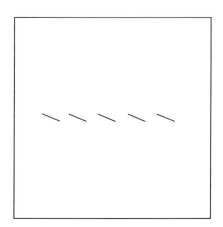

FIG. 22b. *Avoid letting quilting stitches slant.*

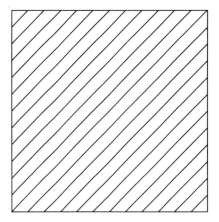

FIG. 23a. *Parallel lines of quilting should be uniformly parallel.*

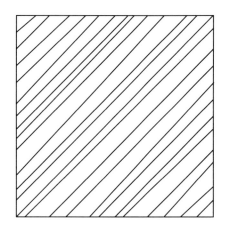

FIG. 23b. *Avoid parallel lines of quilting that are not uniformly distanced or uniformly parallel.*

when the quilt is completed. Judges really aren't concerned with how the quilt was marked, but they do look to see that the marks used to guide quilting stitching do not show and detract from the work. The right marking tools must be carefully selected for each quilt and tested to make certain any visible lines will be removable.

In the overall quilting, there should be no obvious beginnings and endings to the lines, and there should be no knots visible on the top, showing through the top, or on the back. In most cases, a single thread should have been used for the quilting as double threads tend to lend a visually messy look to the work.

The tautness of the quilting stitches should be consistent: tight enough to do

"Competition isn't for everyone, but it has taught me to do my very best, and it has also shown me that sometimes even that isn't good enough."

AUDREE L. SELLS
AQS Show Winner

FIG. 24. *Avoid "herringbone-type pulling" between parallel lines of quilting.*

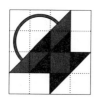

their job but not so tight as to cause distortion. Loose stitches, incompletely stitched areas, or traveling stitches on the top, visible through the top or on the back can all cause visual and technical problems.

The quilt should lie flat with no bubbles, pleats, or extra fullness quilted in. The quilting should not have caused stretching, which usually manifests itself as a "bellied" area in the body of the quilt.

One comment that judges frequently find themselves making when evaluating this area is that the piece needs more quilting. By this the judges mean that, for either design or technical reasons, the quilt should have been more heavily quilted. This frequently means that the piece needs background quilting to support both the top design and the rest of the quilting design and to exploit these to their fullest.

If other types of stitches, instead of or in addition to running stitches, are used for the quilting, the judges will check the execution of these. The color of the quilting thread used, whether regular quilting or sewing thread, metallics, or any other threads, is a design decision and should work well with all the other top elements and not overwhelm or distract from the piece. The judges are aware that thread color that blends with the fabric colors tends to make the quilting stitches appear smaller, while thread color that contrasts with the fabric colors tends to make the quilting stitches appear larger, and they take this into consideration during their review.

Any area of an entry that is a potential problem for the quilting, such as layered areas, areas containing multiple seam allowances, and places where heavier fabrics have been incorporated, are checked to be sure that the evenness and size of the quilting stitch have been maintained. All of the quilting stitches in these areas should also appear strong.

In general, when reviewing machine quilting, the same standards apply as those for hand quilting. Machine quilting is evaluated on how well the stitching lines have been controlled, and whether or not inappropriate machine tension has caused problems. Judges also look to see that there are no unsightly blips of bobbin thread on the quilt top or of top thread on the back, and that the stitch length is uniformly maintained, or creatively varied for effect. In judging quilting, the judges are looking at the quilting stitches, which lend themselves to close visual inspection, but they are also considering the overall result of the quilting, the shadows and highlights created by the quilting. These effects are considered in machine quilting as well as in hand quilting.

Judges carry no inbred biases against

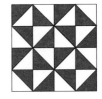

"Enter shows, and go to see them if it is at all possible for you. There is a lot of learning that can be done by just observing."

DAWN E. AMOS
AQS Show Winner

machine quilting. They are concerned with how appropriate the quilting is to the entry and how well it is done. With the improvements in technology and in the skill of quiltmakers, the execution of machine quilting has become an art in itself.

QUILT BACK

Judges do evaluate the backs of quilts, and depending upon the guidelines set up by the sponsors, they also evaluate the backs of wallhangings. With so much backart being employed on today's quilts and wallhangings, the backs of entries frequently provide some delightful surprises

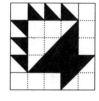

"Don't be discouraged by rejection or not winning – keep trying. Study other winners (and non-winners) to see what makes them special. Talk to other quilters. Be realistic in your evaluation of your work."

ELSIE VREDENBURG

AQS Show Winner

FIG. 26a. *Backing with two evenly spaced seams.*

52

(Figures 25a and 25b, shown on pages 54 and 55).

The fabric used for the backing should be compatible with that used for the top. For traditional backings, major construction seams (if any) should usually be vertical. Generally two evenly spaced seams are preferred over a single seam. The technical reason for this is that any stress will be evenly distributed between the two seams and, aesthetically, it is more visually effective to have two seams evenly spaced on the back (Figures 26a and 26b). However, most judges are willing to accept a single backing seam as long as it is handled well

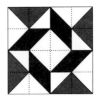

"It is imperative to take your quilting seriously, to be disciplined – otherwise you'll never finish anything. Because you're your own boss, it's easy to let things get in the way of your work."

TERESA TUCKER YOUNG

AQS Show Winner

FIG. 26b. *Backing with a single seam down the center.*

FIG. 25a. *Back of the Best of Show quilt at the 1989 AQS Quilt Show &
Contest:* "Corona II: Solar Eclipse" *by Caryl Bryer Fallert.*

FIG. 25b. *Back of the Best of Show quilt at the 1993 AQS Quilt Show & Contest:* "Air Show" *by Jonathon Shannon.*

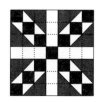

and causes no problems.

Whether the seam allowances on the back are pressed open or to one side does not generally become a matter of concern. If the pressing choice is causing no new problems, either method of handling them is acceptable. What is important, though, is that these seam allowances be consistently pressed open or to one side. They should not be handled in varying methods, nor should the seam allowances be allowed to float from one side to the other along a particular seam.

The backing fabric shouldn't be so overwhelming in print or color that it shadows spottily through the top or changes the color of the quilt top unless this latter is clearly a deliberate design choice. The quilting stitches on the back of the quilt are checked using the same criteria as for those on the top of the quilt; the even penetration of the backing by these stitches is looked at carefully (Figures 27a and 27b).

The entire back should be flat and even. In some cases, backs of wallhangings are checked for hanging devices such as sleeves, loops, etc. These additions should be appropriate for the shape and size of the piece, should be coordinated with the back of the quilt, and should be applied showing good workmanship.

FINISHING OF EDGES

The method used for finishing the edges of the quilt should be suitable to the top design. The finishing of edges can be handled in any number of ways, and the judges will check how well the method chosen is managed.

Whether front over back, back over front, butted, bound, decorative, or in the rare case, raw, edges should be firmly and, usually, unobtrusively stitched. The stitches used, of whatever kind, should be compatible with all the other stitching in the quilt. The edges should be firm and not floppy; the back should not be rolling to the front nor the front rolling to the back.

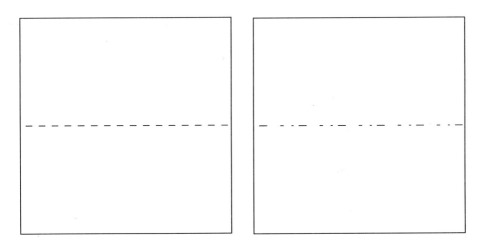

FIG. 27a. *Quilting stitches on back with even penetration.*

FIG. 27b. *Quilting stitches on back with uneven penetration.*

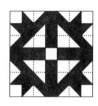

"Completing any quilt never fails to give me a feeling of satisfaction – or is it relief! To win recognition for work I love is even more satisfying."

LUCY BURTSCHI GRADY
AQS Show Winner

All of the edges should be completely and evenly filled with batting. On an entry with straight edges, the edges should remain straight and not waver. If the work is bound, either straight or bias binding is acceptable as long as it conforms to the quilt edges in a smooth fashion and the corners are handled consistently. If bias binding is used, fabric-prepared bias binding is preferred over commercial binding since the latter tends to call undue attention to itself: the color is usually not a true match of the fabrics used in the body of the quilt and rarely is commercial binding of as high a quality.

Any binding or other edge finishing should not appear to be distorted, nor should it distort the outer edges of the quilt. There should not be any bubbles, pleats, or tucks stitched into the outer edges of the quilt top. If the edge finish is a binding, any joints should meet smoothly and the starting and ending meets should be unobtrusive. Also, if the binding is mitered at the corners, the miters should be stitched closed. The thread color used to finish the edges should not distract from the work.

FINISHING OF CORNERS

In addition to checking the finishing technique on the sides of the quilt, the judges also check how well the corners of the quilt are finished. On square or rectangular entries, the corners should meet at ninety-degree angles (Figure 28), being neither dog-eared (Figure 29, page 60) nor cupped (Figure 30, page 60). Care with both the addition of borders and of binding is needed to avoid these problems. Just as in all other parts of the quilt, the workmanship used in finishing the corners of the quilt should be precise.

If the quilt competition allows for novelty entries such as Yo-Yo, Cathedral Window, Biscuit, tied pieces, or other types of traditionally non-quilted pieces, the judges are expected to be generally familiar with these as well as with other types of special

"My quilt was rejected by the first juried show to which it was submitted, but at the next show it was not only accepted for display but was also selected as a prizewinner... no single jury should have the final word on a quilter's work; it really does pay to get a second opinion."

CAROL GODDU
AQS Show Winner

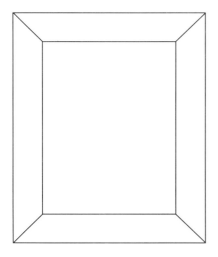

FIG. 28. *Quilt corners should be ninety-degree angles.*

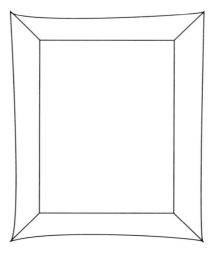

FIG. 29. *Quilt corners should not be dog-eared.*

FIG. 30. *Quilt corners should not be cupped.*

techniques. Each special entry is evaluated based on design, color, general appearance, and the workmanship criteria for that technique.

General Appearance

When considering the General Appearance of the entries, judges determine, first of all, whether the piece meets the requirements of the entry form, of the category in which it is entered, and of the rules and definitions of the particular competition. They check to be sure the entry is free from any major technical or design blunders, presents an integrated, unified look, and that, as far as can be ascertained, it is appropriate for the intended use. They also check to make certain it is neat and clean and not damaged in any way.

"Before sending a quilt for a contest, always use a lint brush on both sides."

JULEE PROSE
AQS Show Winner

The submission should be visually and tactily pleasing and free from bearding (fiber migration), bleeding, crocking, and pilling. At this point the judges also note the complexity of the design, which relates to the visual elements of the work, and the degree of difficulty, which relates to the construction of the piece.

Any use of embellishments or found items should add to and be an integral part of the work and not detract from its overall effectiveness. Of course, judges expect that the entries will be signed and dated even though they are not able to read this information. The show sponsors are responsible for temporarily covering in some way this information. Often during judging the name is covered with a temporarily-stitched-on piece of muslin.

CONCLUSION

The judge, or panel of judges, even though evaluating all of the details of a given entry, are vitally concerned with the quilt as an entire work. They do not hunt aimlessly among the trees and neglect the forest. Their desire is to award recognition to the best designed, best constructed works entered in the competition.

No one aspect is likely to "make or break" a piece. The evaluators are not searching for all the mistakes and errors that they can find in order to disqualify an entry; they are looking for all the positive aspects of the entry that might serve to make it an award winner.

Usually the problem the judges face is not in finding potential winners, but in determining which are the very best of the many good entries – the entries that should earn recognition. Making these decisions can be difficult, especially as the quilts entered in competitions get better all of the time, but judging can be an exciting and satisfying task. While the best quilts win the awards,

"I enjoy the competition and I find awards very meaningful."

MONECA CALVERT
AQS Show Winner

the judges are also rewarded in knowing they have put forth their finest efforts in making those awards (Figure 31).

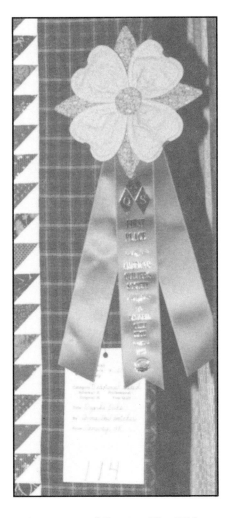

FIG. 31. *Best of Show or Blue Ribbon.*

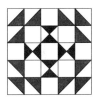

"It is very important to me that my work speaks to others, delighting the eye, or lifting the spirits of those who see it. An award lets me know that with this quilt I have been successful in meeting that goal."

CARYL BRYER FALLERT
AQS Show Winner

SECTION THREE:

In My Judgment Columns

by Patricia J. Morris

Reprinted from *American Quilter*

JUDGING:
THE TOOLS AND THE PROCESS

SPRING 87:
RESPONSIBILITIES OF ENTRANT

it is the responsibility of the entrant to comply with all of the rules of the competition and to fill out the entry form according to the guidelines laid down in the rules.

A quilt competition requires many different things from many different people. The sponsors of the show must have everything well organized and completely planned for, while always staying on their toes to deal with any contingencies that may arise. The judging panel must be prepared to deal professionally and fairly with all the entries. The show staff must be prepared for endless hours of quilt hanging, quilt guarding and show takedown. With all these individuals working hard to do a good job on the show, there yet remains responsibility that belongs to the entrant.

The first responsibility of anyone entering a quilt contest is to read and comply with all of the rules of that contest. While that may sound a bit obvious, it's not always as easy as it sounds. First of all, no two quilt contests work under exactly the same rules, so all of the rules, including the fine print, should be carefully read. But even though the rules may differ from contest to contest, there are some similarities.

Frequently you must indicate on the entry form whether you are a professional in the field of quiltmaking or a hobby/amateur quilter. It really doesn't matter what you personally think your status is when it comes to making this indication on the form. What matters is that particular show's definition of the words "professional" and "amateur." Read the definition carefully and apply it to yourself and then mark the appropriate space on the entry form.

Probably the most important decision the entrant has to make is which category (division, class, whatever the term) a quilt or wallhanging should be entered in. Again, category options differ widely. Generally speaking, though, "Pieced," "Appliqué," and "Mixed Techniques" are used as divisions in a very large number of contests. Deciding whether your quilt is pieced, appliquéd, or uses mixed techniques may seem fairly easy, but it can be tricky. What about a sampler quilt of all appliquéd blocks sashed together? You've used appliqué on the individual blocks but the blocks and sashing were pieced together. In most shows, this quilt would be entered in an appliqué category because that is the predominant technique. The top itself was appliquéd and only the set elements were pieced, therefore it belongs in the appliqué category. But, be sure to carefully read the rules before you mark the category on the entry form.

There are certain quilt patterns that constantly cause problems, such as the Dresden Plate. The individual pieces of this pattern are pieced together into a single unit which is appliquéd to the background. The techniques are nearly equal in their use and generally this quilt belongs in a "Mixed Techniques" division. But only about a third of the time is this done in practice. The other two-thirds of the time Dresden Plate quilts are entered in "Pieced" or "Appliqué" categories.

The "Mixed Techniques" category includes quilts using more than one technique in their top construction, and can also include quilts made using techniques that aren't covered in any other category. "Mixed Techniques" can be a miscellaneous grouping. Read the definitions of the categories carefully so you will know just exactly what "Mixed Techniques" can include for the particular show you are entering.

When you fill out an entry form for a quilt contest, read all of the rules carefully and mark the entry form as required by the rules for that specific contest. Just as the others involved in the quilt contest have their own duties and responsibilities to meet, it is the responsibility of the entrant to comply with all of the rules of the competition and to fill out the entry form according to the guidelines laid down in the rules.

SUMMER 87
QUILTS WITH DIFFERENT TOP SETS

When I say, "Many different types of quilts are entered in competitions," maybe the first types that come to your mind are traditional and innovative ones. Or perhaps the first types you think of are pieced and appliquéd. But for the moment, let's think of another way that quilts can be divided: the top set. Granted, the division of quilts into groups based on how the top is set is not usually a type you will find on a competition entry form. But nonetheless, every quilt entered in a competition is set together in one way or another. And at some point in the evaluation of every entry, the judges must consider the top set.

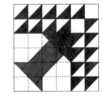

Consideration of a top set involves aspects of both design and workmanship.

As with judging as a whole, the consideration of a top set involves aspects of both design and workmanship. First of all, is the set chosen appropriate to the other elements of the quilt top, and then, how well is the chosen set handled technically? Just as quilt judges probably see more pieced or appliquéd quilts than any other, so they see certain types of sets more often than they see others.

One of the more common sets is butted blocks where every block in the quilt top is a pattern block. Another common set is the alternate plain block set where the pattern blocks are separated by solid, empty blocks. Also, a very popular set is the sashed (lattice work/stripping) quilt top where the pattern blocks are separated by strips of fabric. Of course, there are many other sets possible, some of which do not even involve blocks at all, but the three mentioned seem to be seen most often.

It's important in a butted block set that all the blocks meet in sharp corners, that the proper color thread is used, and that the seam allowances are consistently handled. The seams that join the butted blocks should go straight across the quilt or down or diagonally. In an alternate plain block set, all the blocks should meet in sharp corners, the proper color thread should be used, and the seam allowances should be consistently handled. The seams that join the plain and the pattern blocks of an alternate plain block set should go straight across the quilt or down or diagonally. In a quilt top that has the pattern blocks sashed (lattice/stripping) together, the sashing should be cut the exact width, the grain should be carefully handled, the sashing shouldn't ripple or have tucks or pleats, every meeting of corners should be exact, the proper color of thread should be used, and again the seam allowances should be consistently handled. As before, the sashing that joins the pattern blocks should be straight, whether running straight across or down the quilt, or running diagonally; it shouldn't wobble.

The most common reason why sashing wobbles or why seams joining the blocks of a butted block set or an alternate plain block set are not straight, is that the blocks being joined are not uniform in size. In any set, therefore, the uniformity of the block size is very important. To help keep those seams straight and to help keep sashing from wobbling, be certain all of the blocks are the same size before they are joined.

So, even though quilt competitions don't choose entry categories based on the types of quilt sets, the setting of the quilt top is still important in judging. Whether the quilt is set using one of the common settings already discussed, or is set with a more unusual choice, the setting becomes an integral part of that quilt, contributing to its success.

WINTER **87**
COMMENT SHEETS

From time to time in *American Quilter* columns, I've discussed the comment sheet and some of the types of comments that are written on it. Let's take a closer look at comment sheets, both for those who are familiar with them and those who have no idea of what they are.

First of all, comment sheets are one part of the elimination method of judging a quilt competition. They come in many sizes, may be completely blank or may have a short checklist printed on them. They all have a space for filling in the entry number. Some comment sheets have general statements at the top such as "In their evaluation of your entry, the judges made the following observations." Others may split the comment sheet into two parts with a statement for each part such as "The judges noted these successful areas of your entry" and "The judges noted these problem areas on your entry" or words to that effect. But whatever their size and whatever may or may not be printed on them, the comment sheets are a vehicle for transmitting the observation of the judges to the entrant.

The purpose of the comment sheets is to convey to the entrant exactly which portions of the quiltmaking are being handled

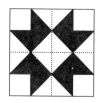

The purpose of the comment sheets is to convey to the entrant exactly which portions of the quiltmaking are being handled well and which areas need improvement.

well and which areas need improvement. This extends a quilt competition beyond the awarding of prizes, whether ribbons or cash. The judges take on some responsibility for upholding high standards of design and workmanship in the craft and instructing entrants on where they are meeting the standards and where their quiltmaking can be improved.

The judges' comment sheets are filled out at the time the entries are evaluated. At a very small show it would be possible, but not preferable, for the judges to fill out the comment sheets themselves as the judging progresses. But, this breaks the judge's concentration, is awkward and distracting, and uses up the time allotted for the judging. Usually one of the assistants is available to record the judges' comments on the comment sheets. This aide is called a scribe. A scribe has to write quickly but legibly, must be able to understand and write down the judge's words, and must abide by an iron-clad rule to respect the confidentiality of the judging process.

When the scribe is working with a single judge, whatever the judge dictates is copied down on the comment sheet. When the scribe is working with a panel of judges, the head judge is the voice of the judges and dictates all of the judges' comments to the scribe. In this way, the scribe listens only for one voice and blocks out the others to avoid confusion.

At breaks during the judging process and in the evening, the judge or the panel of judges read over each comment sheet to be certain that the comments properly reflect their sentiments, that there are no errors, and that the comments are understandable. If there is any problem on a comment sheet, the quilt is brought back so the comment sheet can be corrected. After the judges are satisfied with the comment sheets, they sign or initial them. This whole process does require that the judges have good memories for the quilts they have just evaluated and for what they said about these quilts.

The comment sheets are returned to the entrants at the time the entry is returned, either by mail or in person. They are intended to be helpful to the entrant in future quiltmaking endeavors by supplying an objective evaluation of the entry submitted in the competition.

SUMMER 88

WHAT JUDGES LOOK FOR

When you were a child, did you have scary nightmares about ugly, frightening monsters? Probably at one time or another, most of us have had this experience. In fact, some people don't outgrow their tendencies toward horrific goblins; they just grow up to be quiltmakers and dream about quilt judges!

To hear (or to be more precise, to over-hear) some quiltmakers talking, you'd think every judge had 62 eyes, each equipped with a Sherlock Holmes-type magnifying glass (all those judges, that is, who aren't considered blind by the entrants). Every judge also has six hands, each with a ruler in it. I've heard "The judges don't like pink, there's not one pink quilt that has a ribbon"; "The judges certainly like appliqué a lot better than piecing 'cause all the top ribbons are on appliqué quilts," and many other comments in the same vein.

Entrants and show attendees need to keep in mind that the judges don't zero in on just one tiny detail and then scream, "Out, Ugly Quilt!" if that detail isn't perfect. The judges, of course, look at details, at all the details: the point meets of piecing, how well the appliqué is turned under, the evenness of the quilting stitches, and on and on,

Judges are not attempting to find all of the details that somehow or other are not perfect. What the judges are doing is looking for what is right with the entry.

detail after detail. But, unless one of these details is causing the quilt to fall apart, not one of them will make or break the quilt's chances for an award in the judge's eyes. It is these details combined with the overall impact of the entry that will determine its success or failure in the awards stakes.

An award-winning quilt will be well designed and well executed. The entire entry will "hang together" to present a unified, integrated statement. The details of the design and execution should contribute toward the unity of the piece.

Judges are not attempting to find all of the details that somehow or other are not perfect. What the judges are doing is looking for what is right with the entry. They are trying to identify all the details that are well handled from both a design and workmanship point of view. They are trying to assess the impact of the entire piece and to determine how well a given work stands up against its competition. Judges do not gather around an entry and shout with glee whenever some less than perfect detail comes into view.

An award on a quilt neither signifies an overzealous use of magnifier and ruler by the judges, nor denotes a personal prejudice shared by the judges. An award on a quilt means that in a given category, all things considered, this was the best entry.

WINTER 89
THOSE WHO SERVE AS JUDGES

Quiltmakers enter competitions for many valid reasons. And they enter all kinds of competitions: those sponsored by their local guilds, county and state fairs, regional and national contests plus a wide variety of others. While competitions may vary in their entry requirements, categories, and awards, one thing is constant: a judge or judges will be used to determine competition winners.

But just who are these judges? Of course it comes to mind that the contest will be judged by quilt judges. However, judges come to competitions with different backgrounds, different experiences and therefore, different perspectives.

Judges come to competitions with different backgrounds, different experiences and therefore, different perspectives.

Some judges may be quilt shop or fabric store owners. They are most familiar with the tools, materials and equipment of the field and are adept at dealing tactfully with the general public.

Judges who are quiltmaking teachers are knowledgeable in the field and are often asked to bring this ability to bear in the judging forum.

Artists are sometimes invited to be members of a judging panel. While they may not be experts on quilts as such and, in fact, may have little familiarity with them, they are able to evaluate the design, color, composition and other intrinsic elements even if they are not conversant with the technical details.

Those who write about quilts are often chosen to work as judges because of their breadth of information about the field.

Others invited to serve on judging panels may work in fields which incidentally touch quiltmaking. For instance, home economics teachers may teach an occasional section of quiltmaking and on the basis of this be considered for show judging. Likewise a textile expert of a historical society maybe asked to judge shows because of his/her contact with quilts within the scope of that profession.

In addition to the above-mentioned individuals are quilt judges who have devoted a great deal of effort to the study of quilt judging and are found on the evaluation panels for judged and juried shows. These experienced quilt judges may also be shop owners, quiltmaking teachers and so forth. Quilt judging is a relatively small field and individuals frequently choose to pursue more than one path through it.

Generally speaking, show sponsors try to balance the strengths of those serving on the judging panel in order to provide the strongest team possible to evaluate their competitions. If it's important to you to know the makeup of the judging panel (or the background of the single judge who will be making the awards), check the entry form and the contest rules. The judges are sometimes listed there. In other cases, the judges are named in the show catalog along with a brief biography or possibly a statement by each judge. Often, too, the grapevine will bring word as to who will be judging which shows. If it seems very important to you to know who the judges will be, a little research on your part will generally get you the names and backgrounds.

SPRING 90

IS IT IMPORTANT TO KNOW WHO THE
JUDGES ARE?

*Don't try to quilt to your
perceptions of the judge or
judges....Trust the show
sponsors to have chosen a
professional judging
team who will give every
entry a fair and equitable
evaluation.*

I have discussed the types of individuals who judge quilt competitions. They may be experienced quilt judges or may be experts in other areas either directly related or relatively unrelated to quiltmaking.

Is it important to know who will judge a given show? Some quilters feel it is very important to know who will be judging a contest before they will even consider entering. Other entrants could care less who will be judging a show and enter the competition for reasons unrelated to the judges.

Objectively, though, is it important to know who will be the judges? Will it make any real difference to a given entry or entrant? Probably not, at least I would sincerely trust and hope not. Remember that a quilter puts an entry in a specific show and is not making an entry to a specific person. The quilter's entry must meet the contest requirements and when it does, it is the panel of judges that determines the winner, not a single judge. When there is only one judge, entrants can get a bit nervous about any biases that judge may have. But by and large, a knowledgeable and experienced quilt judge, acting in a professional manner, is capable of putting aside biases and objectively addressing the responsibilities at hand.

Yet you still have your doubts, right? If you read that Anne Appliqué, Betty Batting, and Carol Color are judging a show you are considering entering, does it make you deliriously happy or make you rethink entering? Be very aware that while these three judges work together on a competition, it's no longer Anne, Betty, and Carol, but a fourth entity emerges that is a composite of these three: Trudy Team. (Of course, I am supposing that these three individuals are working smoothly together with nary a prima donna in the bunch.)

What about the competition you read about and decide to enter, and then find has as its judge Susie Supermod? Do you make sure you use an innovative design combined with today's fabrics and done entirely on your machine? Is that really fair to Susie, the judge, or even more importantly, to yourself? It is certainly no more fair than making a hand constructed, traditional design in reproduction fabrics if you know that Tessie Traditional is the judge. It is always a bad idea to quilt to your conception of a judge's preferences. First and most importantly, it's a bad idea because the judge won't be displaying preferences during the judging, and secondly, because you may have the judge pegged wrong. It doesn't matter what style the judge may choose for personal work since this has no relation to choosing award winners in a competition.

In seeking to balance a team of judges, some show sponsors may select judges based on a perception of the judge's bent as well as the judge's knowledge, experience, and expertise. But the sponsors, too, can have the judge pegged wrong. I think I have sometimes been asked to be a member of a judging panel because I really am such a traditionalist. Conversely, I sense I have also been asked to be a member of a judging panel because I really like that "way-out new stuff." And I positively know that on occasion I have been asked to be a member of a panel to be the balancing judge between two judges, one of whom is perceived as a traditionalist and the other of whom is considered avante-garde!

When it comes to entering quilt competitions, do yourself a favor: don't try to quilt to your perceptions of the judge or judges. Study the entrance requirements and submit a piece that will meet these. Trust the show sponsors to have chosen a professional judging team who will give every entry a fair and equitable evaluation.

SUMMER 90

CRITERIA FOR JUDGING

When preparing to enter a work in a quilt competition, there are certain givens: the entrant has to follow the rules of the particular contest, send the application form (and whatever else is required) by the stated deadline, and so forth. These details are carefully set out in the competition rules and are usually easy to understand and comply with. Problems tend to pop up when the entrants look for the same kind of detailed, clear-cut listing of "Always" and "Never" items that the judges will use when evaluating entries. Judging a competition would certainly be easier if there were such a list of items with which to work, but nothing like this is available.

Actually, there are very few "Always" and "Never" details in judging quilts and a tremendous number of "It All Depends."

Actually, there are very few "Always" and "Never" details in judging quilts and a tremendous number of "It All Depends." The most obvious "Always" and "Never" details are: 1) "Always" follow the entry rules; 2) "Always" be sure the entry is clean. ("Never" enter a dirty quilt or hanging.) Beyond these, the judges are mainly working in the area of "It All Depends." As to what winning "Depends" on, the answer is straightforward: it "Depends" on how well the design works and on how well the technical aspects uphold the design.

It would be terribly unfair to say entries must "Always" have borders and that the corners of the borders can "Never" be handled in any way other than by mitering. For some entries, a border isn't needed at all and might detract from the work. For other entries a border is just fine, but the border design might be ruined if it had to be mitered. For still other entries, a mitered border is the perfect touch. Whether or not a border should be mitered "Depends" on the specific entry the judges are considering.

This doesn't mean that the judges are not applying firm criteria to the items being evaluated – they are. They expect the work to be well integrated, the design to be effective, and the technical aspects to be well done. But the quiltmaker has to be allowed to arrive at this end result without an unrealistic listing of "Always" and "Never" that could seriously interfere with the creative and technical aspects of the work.

Probably the best guide is to remember that no one thing is likely to make or break an entry's chances in a competition. It is the individual details, and these in combination with the overall impact that is of prime consideration during the evaluation process. Details handled well will lead to recognition of the piece, even if one of these details is less than perfect.

So, although a list of "Always" and

"Never" items would seem to be desirable, it would be neither fair nor realistic. It's the "Depends" that separate the award winners from the other entries in a juried competition.

SPRING 92

LETTING GO OF JUDGING MYTHS

Somehow these mythical rules have crept into the subconscious of an unbelievably large number of quilters.

In discussing the subject of quilt judging, one must first face the difficult task of getting past the tales of what "they" like, what "they" insist on, what "they" say must be done. "They," of course, are those mysterious, fictional judges who ran around at the dawn of quiltmaking setting up arbitrary, unrealistic and ironclad rules about what award-winning quilts must be. Somehow these mythical rules have crept into the subconscious of an unbelievably large number of quilters. Time after time these nonexistent rules have been cited as written in blood or carved in stone.

In taking a closer look at these impossibly strict, if nonexistent, rules, perhaps we can throw some light on them. First is the idea that all the good quilts – the best quilts, the winning quilts, the real quilts – are totally hand done. This is simply not the case. There are many excellent machine-made quilts, just as there are many excellent handmade quilts. In both cases some have and some have not received awards. There are also poorly made machine quilts just as there are poorly made hand quilts. Neither the machine-making nor the hand-making in itself confers excellence or disaster on a quilt.

I was told in a recent letter that when judges look at hand-pieced, hand-quilted quilts, they are very strict about borders being mitered, stitches being tiny and points touching. To take these in reverse order, yes, the points should meet accurately. Yes, the stitches should be small enough to hold the pieces together, but what degree of tininess is required, my correspondent did not define. In fact, if the pieces are held firmly together, the question of stitch size need never arise. As for the borders, they may be mitered, but they may also go straight across, go straight down, have set-in corners, have decorative corners or feature any kind of treatment the imaginative mind of the quiltmaker can devise. Judges will be checking to see if the design of the border is compatible with, and complementary to, the design of the top. They will be checking to see that the border is well handled technically. At no point will they demand mitering. And as for strictness, I'd prefer to think that when judges look at entries they are not strict, but rather, very thorough and very fair.

Judges do not invent arbitrary rules that have no relevance to the task of judging – recognizing the well-designed, well-executed work of quiltmaking art. I have been asked whether judges, when they look at machine-pieced quilts, insist that the piecing be done "properly" (not sewn into the seam allowances but stopped ¼" before the raw edge), just as they do for hand-pieced work. I've evaluated a lot of hand- and machine-pieced entries over the years and worked at this assignment with many different quilt judges. Never once has the subject of where the seam line should start and stop been discussed. True, I've heard teachers discussing this subject, but never judges. If there is no problem in an area, why would any attention be paid to where the seam line starts and stops? If there is a problem, how can the judges be absolutely certain of the cause, looking at just the outside? On no entry, whether hand- or machine-pieced, has this been a matter of concern.

The result of all these mysterious, nonexistent judging rules is to set up unrealistic standards, and then to demand perfection in attaining them. I've never seen a perfect quilt, and frankly, never expect to see one. However, I am equally certain that I will continue to see more awe-inspiring quilt designs supported by excellent construction. And, looking at all entries, I will try to be as thorough, as fair, and – most importantly – as realistic as possible in recognizing the best entries in the competition. I will also entirely put out of my mind even the memory of some of these mysterious rules I hear about from time to time.

SPECIFICS ON MATERIALS, TECHNIQUES & PROBLEMS

FALL 85
THE MARKING OF QUILTING LINES

Judging a quilt competition provides a special challenge. It requires total concentration, the ability to think on your feet, to make decisions, and above all to maintain objectivity. Of course, the higher the quality of the entries, the more exacting becomes the challenge for a judge, or a panel of judges, to determine the best submission in each category.

As the judge works through the quilts submitted in a contest, the strongest elements of each quilt demand recognition. At the same time, the problems of each quilt stand out. There are some problems that appear again and again in any given competition. These problems keep turning up as the judge evaluates competition after competition.

One of the biggest recurring problems is caused by the instrument used to mark the quilting design on the quilt top. Most often the instrument used has been a pencil and time after time the judge says "pencil marks" as a comment for the critique sheet. It's important to remember that if a pencil is used for marking the quilt design, it should

One of the biggest recurring problems is caused by the instrument used to mark the quilting design on the quilt top.

be used with a very light hand. After the quilting is completed, if any of the pencil lines are still visible, they should be removed.

Pencil marks are not the only causes of the marking problem as frequently marks are still on the quilt from the use of a water soluble pen. If you feel you do want to use a wash-out marker, and the advisability of this is questionable, be sure to follow the directions exactly and remove all the marks completely. Certain marking tools, such as a ball-point pen, are always unacceptable.

Whatever reason you have for making quilts, whether you are submitting them in competitions or not, be extremely cautious when marking your quilting design and remove all marks, of whatever type, once the quilting is completed.

WINTER 85
THREAD USED FOR PIECING

When judging a quilt competition, it's amazing how much information you can get about the quiltmaker and the quiltmaker's working habits just from looking at the quilt a person has made.

Most quiltmakers are very careful to have all the tools and supplies they will need on hand when they are getting ready to begin a new pieced quilt. This involves, of course, the fabric, templates, pencils, scissors, needles, thimbles, and thread. It may also involve any number of other gadgets, notions and time savers of all kinds.

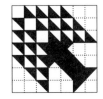

Whether you're submitting your quilt for competition or not, the principle remains the same: thread color for piecing should match fabric color.

Usually the quiltmaker is very careful when choosing these items to get the best fabric available in the desired range of colors, whether they be solids or prints. All the pencils and scissors get sharpened and tested, the templates are exact, a new package of needles is ready and the thimble fits comfortably. Then, and it happens more often than you'd believe, the quiltmaker grabs a spool of thread and starts to piece the quilt.

Notice I said "grabs a spool of thread," and that means whatever comes first to hand. Most often it turns out to be white or off-white. This is terrific if the fabrics you are piecing happen to be white or off-white.

Unfortunately, this is not always the case. Frequently the fabrics are red, blue, orange, or green and the white or off-white thread has been used to piece them together. When this quilt shows up in a competition, the judges will be certain to make the comment "Thread color for piecing should match the fabric color."

I realize that theoretically the thread used for piecing should not show in the completed quilt. After all, the piecing is done from the wrong side and all that thread should rest against the batting. In actual practice, however, the thread does show. The reasons that it shows are varied: the stitching isn't tight enough, the stitching line isn't straight enough, the pressing job could have been better, the quilting is stressing the seam line, and so forth. Actually, it doesn't matter why it might show; it just does in an overwhelming number of quilts. When the thread that shows is a color that doesn't match the fabric color, the judges will comment. It's advisable to check your thread supply against your chosen fabrics before beginning your piecing. If the thread colors you have on hand don't match your fabrics, a quick trip to the local quilt shop is in order. Whether you're submitting your quilt for competition or not, the principle remains the same: thread color for piecing should match fabric color.

SPRING 88
EDGE FINISHING

Quiltmaking is a process that involves the use of many different techniques and steps. Quiltmakers refer to piecing, appliqué and quilting as examples of some of the construction techniques that are used in quiltmaking. Quiltmakers also break down the process into designing the quilt, drafting the pattern and making the templates, fabric preparation, sewing and quilting. But as you listen to the various breakdowns that quiltmakers use in discussing the making of a quilt, one step or technique is rarely mentioned. That step is edge finishing. And when judging quilt competitions it becomes very clear (painfully clear at times) that it is seldom mentioned because seldom is much real care lavished on edge finishing. Sometimes the edge finishing seems to be an afterthought on the part of the maker as something that has to be done because you can't use a quilt with open edges.

Judges who are evaluating the submissions in a quilt competition frequently run across different kinds of problems with the edge finishings. Among these is the problem of batting. The batting should always come evenly all the way out to the outsides of the quilt. There shouldn't be thin areas that have little or no batting, and there

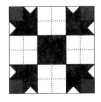

Even if you are not entering a competition, your edge finishing should be as carefully handled as every other part of your quilt.

shouldn't be thick areas where excess batting has been crunched in instead of being trimmed away. The outside edges of the quilt should be as firm and even with batting as the main body of the quilt.

Another problem that keeps popping up is the corners of the quilt. Whatever edge finishing method the quiltmaker chooses to use, the difficulty of getting good corners must be overcome. Square corners should remain square and rounded corners should be smoothly rounded. The square corners should be ninety-degree angles in every case and if the four corners are rounded, all four corners should use the same arc. The corner, no matter what type, should not be distorted by the edge finishing, and it should lie flat.

One of the most popular edge finishing methods is the use of binding. If binding is used, it should be carefully applied. The binding should turn the corners neatly whether those corners are square or rounded. If a miter is used at a corner, it should be a neat one and it should be stitched closed. Unfortunately, many times stretching and pulling has occurred during the binding application, and the binding and/or the border will have pulls or pleats or be distorted in some way. If binding is used, it is almost always much more successful if it has been cut from fabric as opposed to being a commercial binding which can tend to call unwanted attention to itself because of its quality or color. Any joins in the binding should be smooth and unobtrusive.

No matter which edge finishing is chosen, good stitching techniques should be used. The thread used in edge finishing should match the color of the fabric used.

The judges for a competition are aware of the pitfalls of edge finishing, and the entrant must be aware of these pitfalls too, and should work to avoid them. If you are entering a competition, you don't want your work to fail because of a poor job of edge finishing. Even if you are not entering a competition, your edge finishing should be as carefully handled as every other part of your quilt. Edge finishing should be an integral part of the process of making a quilt and not just an afterthought.

WINTER 88
MATERIALS USED

It isn't only how the quilt was made and the design chosen that can affect the evaluation of an entry. What was used to make the quilt is also important.

We know that judges of a quilt competition are expected to give each entry a fair and equitable evaluation which means, of course, that they will take a careful look at the workmanship of each piece. Along with the workmanship, design is very important, as well as the use of color in the interpretation of the design. However, there is another element that judges must look at and that is: what materials were used to make the quilt.

In the majority of quilt shows across the country, the competition rules state that the entries must be made of fabric. Therefore, when the subject is what was used to make the quilt, fabric is the main topic. Does it seem strange that the judges take into account the fabric used to make the quilt? Not if you remember that the judges judge the total quilt, not just how it was made.

First, the fabric is checked to be sure it is suitable to the design. With seemingly endless designs available, the fabric can be anything from the most widely used (cottons) to tiny bits of specialty fabrics (maybe leather or whatever) that highlight details and are most usually found in wall quilts. The fabric used can be nearly any kind of fabric, but generally, cottons and blends predominate in bed quilts while the more special and unusual fabrics get their greatest use in wall quilts.

Just as the workmanship is checked to be sure it is going to wear well over the long haul, so too is the fabric checked to be sure it is going to hold up. This means that judges expect to see a reasonably good quality of fabric used in the entries being evaluated. Unfortunately, some quiltmakers use poor quality fabrics for their work. This is especially the case with quilt backings, some of which seem little better than cheesecloth. And sometimes even the fabrics used in the quilt top could be of better quality. It is very disappointing to see a wonderfully designed and well executed quilt made up in second rate fabric. It means that a great deal of time and effort has been spent on a quilt that will have a much shorter life span than if a good quality fabric has been used.

Obviously, given the costs of today's fabrics, the judges are not unrealistic about the fabrics. They do not expect expensive designer fabrics to be used. But they do expect to find a relatively good quality of fabrics in the entries they evaluate.

Therefore, it isn't only how the quilt was made and the design chosen that can affect the evaluation of an entry. What was used to make the quilt is also important.

SPRING 89
QUILTING THREAD COLOR

The choice of quilting thread color is just one more design decision that faces the quiltmaker, and nowhere are there rules about what choices should be made.

When judges are in the process of evaluating entries, the well-designed and well-executed work of the quiltmaker's art is what they are looking for. One facet of the entries to be evaluated is color, which is intimately linked to the overall design of the work. In this case, the color of the fabric becomes the focus of attention.

There is another side to the color story which is seldom mentioned but that is of concern to the quiltmaker. This is the color of thread used to quilt the work. It's amazing how many underground rumors fly concerning the quilting thread color: "Judges only permit the use of white or off-white quilting thread," "You are never allowed to use more than one color of quilting thread on a project," "The color of the quilting thread must match the color of the backing." I've heard all of the above plus others, and they're all untrue. I have never heard any of these opinions from a quilt judge – only from quiltmakers who are trying to second-guess the judges.

The quiltmaker chooses the quilting thread color, and that is a design decision. Now, the judges for a given competition may feel that the quiltmaker could have made a better choice for that particular quilt, but there is no "always, never, must, or can't" involved. The color should enhance and highlight the top design. Just as the quilting adds another design element to the quilt, so too does the thread color. Even colored metallic threads can be used for quilting, adding another complication and point of interest to the work.

Just as there are design reasons for choosing certain colored quilting threads, there may also be an apparently technical reason for choosing them. When the color of the quilting thread matches the color of the fabric, the quilting stitches appear to be smaller than when the color of the quilting thread contrasts with the fabric. So if the quiltmaker wishes the quilting stitches to seem smaller than they really are, the choice will be to use the color of quilting thread that matches the fabric.

Some quiltmakers feel that the use of different colors of quilting thread makes the back messy. Some even choose a print backing to avoid drawing attention to the thread colors. This is an acceptable choice, but so is a solid color backing, since the quilting thread colors can provide additional design interest to the back of the quilt.

The choice of quilting thread color is just one more design decision that faces the quiltmaker, and nowhere are there rules about what choices should be made.

FALL 90
PIECES THAT DON'T INTEGRATE

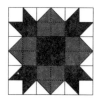

At each stage in the making
of a quilt it's important to
keep in focus how well the
piece is integrated,
how well it hangs together,
and how well it presents
a statement.

In the process of judging a quilt competition, the judge or judging panel evaluates "X" number of entries depending on the size of the show. Let's say this hypothetical quilt show has one hundred entries, all of them bed quilts. An evaluation in this instance can be a smooth one or it can become complicated. One thing that makes judging smoother is if the judges have just one hundred quilts to look at in this show and not one hundred that become one hundred and fifty or more. No, this is not double talk or sloppy mathematics, but a very real problem of a single quilt's being two works and in some cases, three.

It is not an unusual thing for the judges to look at a quilt and see a terrific border and a very good central area. However, this border and this central area may have absolutely no relationship to one another. The colors, the fabrics, the design elements may lead separate lives in each of these areas. In some cases, it will appear as if there has been an attempt to enlarge the piece by adding the borders, and the relationship among the elements was of only the slightest concern. At other times, the judges may be totally baffled as to why the two parts of the entry are so different. Of course, the "why" is really unimportant to the judges, whose job is to recognize the best pieces entered and not to try to figure out why the entry seems made up of parts of different quilts. But it can be truly puzzling.

Obviously, one quilt's seeming like two isn't always a matter of enlargement. Most often the entire quilt was planned this way and the problem developed when what should have worked as a color/fabric/design element in the border just didn't make it. This is simply one of the hazards, but also one of the challenges of quiltmaking. It is very important that the completed item be an integrated work. All of the aspects must "hang together."

Of course, it isn't always just a matter of one entry's seeming to be two entries because the central area and the border look as if they belong to two different quilts. Sometimes the set, whether it be block to block, alternate plain blocks, or sashing (or some other) seems to "not go with" or "take away from" the blocks. Other times the quilting design appears to live a life independent of the quilt top design. Frequently, this matter of elements looking like parts of different quilts is manifested in a mixed-technique entry. By definition a mixed-technique category is for those entries using more than one quiltmaking technique, most often a mix of piecing and appliqué. Sometimes the judges find themselves evaluating a work with precise piecing and excellent appliqué but with design elements using these two techniques that don't seem to have even a nodding acquaintance. This is always a matter of disappointment for the judges, who once again have to note on a comment sheet, "The elements of the work could be better integrated" or a similar phrase.

At each stage in the making of a quilt it's important to keep in focus how well the piece is integrated, how well it hangs together, and how well it presents a statement. Be sure the piece you make, whether for competition or not, is a unified work.

WINTER 90
CORNER AND SIDE PROBLEMS

When judges evaluate a quilt competition, they look at many different aspects of each entry. This means that with every entry the judges take note of all of these aspects and evaluate their success while at the same time they formulate appropriate comments and determine whether or not the piece is a potential ribbon winner. This does not mean that the judges have to be superhuman; they just have to be careful and observant.

Some problems are obvious because they appear so frequently. Sometimes it seems like an epidemic: all of a sudden a seldom-seen problem starts showing up repeatedly. Entry after entry exhibits the same defect. One current epidemic is a "corner and sides" problem. A quilt or wallhanging that is made to be square or rectangular should have square corners. That means that each of the corners should be ninety-degree angles, or so close to ninety-degree angles that the eye cannot detect a deviation even though a measuring instrument might. All four corners should be the same (unless differing for design purposes). Unfortunately, the current epidemic has brought a large number of entries to the judges' attention that have "dog-ears." The

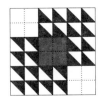

A quilt or wallhanging
that is made to be square or
rectangular should have
square corners.

corners are not ninety-degree angles, so they swoop outwards to points which look very much like a dog's ear. The problem is compounded when all four corners are "dog-eared" to a different degree. Pieces with mitered borders tend to have more "dog-eared" corners than pieces with other kinds of border treatments, but all kinds of corners are subject to this problem. Quilts that have this problem do not look their best when used on a bed, although in this case the viewer usually doesn't see all four problem corners at once. Wallhangings with "dog-eared" corners are at an even bigger disadvantage when displayed. Of course, not all quilts are square or rectangular and even some square and rectangular pieces have curved (or other) corner treatments as design elements. But those corners meant to be square should be ninety-degree angles.

The other part of this "corner and sides" problem is that often (too often) the sides of the quilt are not straight. The outside edges of the work wobble all the way from top to bottom and from side to side. This often happens in conjunction with "dog-eared" corners but can happen even when the corners are precisely handled. It's important to keep the outside edges (of the sides, top, and bottom) totally straight so that when the piece is displayed on a bed or wall it will

show to the best advantage. Also, the wobbly sides can detract from the top design or
from the border design by providing a need-
less distraction. Of course, not all quilts
have straight sides but those that do should
be straight. If a quilt doesn't have a straight
edge but a regularly curved (square,
pointed, etc.) edge, all of the curves
(squares, points, etc.) should extend the
same distance from the body of the piece.
Epidemics, including the "corner and sides"
problem, are things to avoid.

SUMMER 91

QUILTING – DISTRIBUTION AND
TECHNIQUE

*Judges have become
increasingly aware of the
fine points of quilting
design and techniques as
well as the pitfalls.*

These days there are relatively few quilt competitions that make provisions for novelty and special items such as a Cathedral Window quilt or a crazy quilt. Most competitions require that all entries be quilted. This means that judges look at a great deal of piecing, appliqué, and other techniques, but much, much more quilting. Judges have become increasingly aware of the fine points of quilting design and techniques as well as the pitfalls.

One of the pitfalls that frequently seems to arise when entries are evaluated is an insufficiency of quilting. This can mean that there isn't enough quilting to technically hold the three layers of the textile sandwich together. It can also mean that there isn't enough quilting to prevent internal sagging between quilted areas. Further, it can mean that there isn't enough quilting to form a background and highlight the rest of the quilting design and the top design.

Quiltmakers over the past five or six years have become aware of the importance of this background quilting to the overall success of a project. As a consequence, entries in quilt competitions have had more of this vital background quilting.

This is all for the best, but as you might have figured, there has to be a catch: it's also important to do a good job of it. Now that good job is twofold: first, the quilting stitches should be well done, and second, the design of the background needs to be well planned. Also important is consistency in the background quilting, which needs to be maintained over the entire quilt.

There are all kinds of wonderful possibilities for background quilting designs. One of the most often used is the grid of hanging diamonds. In this design, northwest to southeast diagonal lines are used along with northeast to southwest diagonal lines. These lines cross, forming the grid of "hanging diamonds." This grid can be formed of varying degrees of angles, the choice being that of the quiltmaker, as is the choice of how close together the diagonal lines should be quilted and whether they should be single, double or triple lines. All of these are decisions that have to be made before the quilting is started. A vital detail to keep in mind is that the grid must remain true where it starts and ends. It can start and end at the edge finishing, at the border or wherever necessary, but each joint of the hanging diamonds should fall in the same relation to the edge, border or wherever it starts and ends. If the grid does not remain true, the entire quilt will look off balance, as though it were hanging at an angle. This is the illusion created by a grid that does not remain true.

The grid should also be even and the lines equidistant all over the quilt. It is distracting to see a grid where the lines are a half-inch apart in some areas and three-quarters inch to an inch apart in other areas. It is equally distracting to have two lines of quilting which begin an inch apart at one end of the quilt, get closer together across the body of the work, and end up a half-inch apart at the other end of the quilt.

Background quilting is an important part of many quilts and it should always be carefully planned and executed.

WINTER 92

WOBBLING QUILTS

Of the many details that judges look at when evaluating entries in a competition, the wobble factor can be one of the most obvious problems that they encounter. A wobble is any deviation of a straight line from one side to the other. Anywhere there is supposed to be a straight line, there is the potential for a wobble.

If a quilt is composed of blocks that have been joined by sashing, the sashing should run straight and true across the quilt. Unfortunately, many times the sashing seems to swerve first to one side and then to the other. The two most common causes of the resulting wobble are: 1) that the blocks sashed together are not all the same size and the sashing tends to "move" (be pulled) toward the smaller sized blocks, and 2) that there is a significant imbalance in the amount of quilting from one block to the next. The sashing will tend to "move" toward the blocks with the larger amount of quilting. Sashing that wobbles is a definite distraction, no matter how well the other construction details are handled.

It is also possible to have a wobbly border or series of borders. If the center medallion of a quilt or the central design area of a quilt is not absolutely straight, the border or

A wobble is any deviation of a straight line from one side to the other. Anywhere there is supposed to be a straight line, there is the potential for a wobble.

borders that are added will not be straight. In fact, the wobble tends to become more pronounced with the addition of each border. Another problem that can cause the border to wobble is an imbalance of quilting between the center of the quilt and the border area. If the center medallion or the central design area of the quilt is very heavily quilted and the border or borders are only lightly quilted, then the border will tend to pull in toward the center of the quilt and develop a wobble. Also, if the borders aren't carefully measured, cut, and attached there is a possibility of their ending up being less than straight.

Of course, if the sashing isn't straight or the border area isn't straight, then it is highly likely that the outside edges of the piece won't be straight either and the judges will note "edge wobbles" on the comment sheet. It is, however, entirely possible to have dead-straight sashings or block joinings, and straight-as-a-die border or borders and still have edges that wobble. This usually means that the problem lies only with the edge finishing technique.

In addition to the straight lines of the quilt top which are subject to the wobble factor, the lines of quilting are also subject to this same problem. If what is supposed to be a straight line of quilting wanders first to one side and then to the other, it is a definite distraction. The wandering line calls undue attention to itself and takes away from the top design and from the quilting design. In addition to the wobble created when the entire line of quilting swerves from side to side, it is also possible for the individual quilting stitches to wobble, first slanting one way and then another. Again, this distracts from the overall effect of the quilt.

Quiltmakers should be aware of and alert to the wobble factor when they are in the construction process. A quilt that will lie flat and hang square will be free of the wobble factor, a distraction that takes away from the precision of any quilt.

A quilt that will lie flat and hang square will be free of the wobble factor, a distraction that takes away from the precision of any quilt.

INTERPRETING
JUDGES' COMMENTS

SPRING 86
"BASIC TECHNIQUES NEED WORK" –
PIECING

When working a pieced quilt for entry in a competition, or for any other purpose, remember to concentrate on your piecing skills. Improve them, whether you use hand piecing or machine piecing techniques.

Most quiltmakers begin making quilts by learning how to piece, appliqué and quilt. These are usually considered the three basic techniques. Beyond these lie various other techniques and refinements, but it would seem safe to assume that most quiltmakers have relatively good control over the basic techniques.

Yet, over and over again you will hear judges making the comment "basic techniques need improvement." Granted, this is a fairly broad statement, yet what it often boils down to is that the piecing, or the appliqué, or the quilting on a given entry needs to be better done. It can mean that there are so many problems with the basic techniques that the judges cannot make a comment on each individual problem, but must resort to this general statement.

Let's take a look at what this general statement means in relation to the particular technique of piecing. The first and most obvious requirement in piecing is that at any point where seams meet, they should meet exactly, regardless of the number of seams converging. In other words for a four patch, all four pieces must meet exactly and for the center of an eight-pointed star, all eight of the diamond points must meet exactly, and so on. This is the first requirement for piecing, and meeting or not meeting this requirement will make or break the quilt top in the judge's eyes.

The seam lines should be sewn straight on straight edged pieces while for curved pieces, the seam lines should be smoothly curved without any flat areas, pointed areas, gathers or puckers. The seam allowances on a pieced top should lie flat and not cause a problem along the seam or be bulky in the area where many seams meet or cross. The seam allowances should not shadow through the top as little lines of darker color but should be trimmed and graded where necessary.

All of the points or corners of every triangle and diamond should be complete and not chopped off or blunted. Every piece in the quilt top should be cut in relation to the grain of the fabric and positioned in the top in relation to the grain. The judges will be looking for consistency and/or logic in the use of grain.

Whenever the pieced top is made up of individual blocks, it is vital that all be the same size. If they aren't, it will be apparent very soon as deviations in block size will cause the block seams or sashing strips to wobble. This problem shows up most frequently on pieced sampler quilts and less frequently on pieced quilts where each block is made with the same pattern.

The thread used to piece the top should match the color of fabric. The stitches used should be small and close together and tightly enough sewn so that the seam line is firmly held. The tension of the stitching should be consistent. It doesn't matter whether these seams are sewn by hand or by machine, what does matter is how well they are sewn. The entire top of the quilt should lie flat without any distortions caused by the piecing technique.

Occasionally, the judges will make a comment on one or another of the above points in piecing, but when they run across an entry that has problems in many of the areas discussed above, you may get the comment "basic techniques need improvement." In this case, it is the basic technique of piecing that needs improvement.

When working on a pieced quilt for entry in a competition, or for any other purpose, remember to concentrate on your piecing skills. Improve them, whether you use hand piecing or machine piecing techniques. It's only by doing this that you will avoid hearing from a judge (or from that little voice in the back of your mind) that your basic techniques need improvement.

SUMMER 86
"BASIC TECHNIQUES NEED WORK" –
APPLIQUÉ

Sometimes when a judge looks at an entry in an appliqué category, there are just so many problems visible that it would be prohibitive in terms of time to enumerate them all on the comment sheet. Also, a long list of this type would probably be crushing to an entrant. So the sentence "basic techniques need improvement" comes into play. For the judge, it covers the multitude of problems exhibited in the entry and for the maker it indicates a need to brush up on all of the details that go into executing good appliqué.

First of all, all background blocks should be uniform in size and have the grain lying in the same direction. The grain of the appliqué pieces should have been employed in accordance with some logic and consistency and not haphazardly. All of the appliqué pieces should lie flat on the background block with no distortions or bulges. There should be no raw edges and no frays in evidence and all basting should have been removed (honest, some quilt-makers forget to take basting stitches out). All of the curves on the appliqué pieces should be smooth and all of the outside points should be sharply pointed. The

If the comment sheet for an appliqué quilt entry includes the sentence "Basic techniques need improvement,"... it's time to go back to the basics and brush up on all of the elements of the appliqué technique and work at perfecting each of them.

inside points should be sharp and tightly stitched with no frayed threads. Shapes of the individual appliqué pieces should be uniformly maintained. For instance, if there are eight identical leaves in a given block, all eight leaves should be as nearly identical in size and shape as possible.

When looking at the appliqué pieces, the judge does not want to see pencil lines (or the residue of other marking tools) on top of the appliquéd piece or along the edge of the piece. This turning guide line should be under the appliqué piece. There should be no "shadowing through" of darker color appliqués underlying lighter color appliqués. This is one of the problems so frequently seen in appliqué work. If you are making a "Sunbonnet Sue" who is wearing a dark green dress with a light yellow apron over it, be sure to cut away the area of the dress that lies under the apron, or underline the apron to avoid "shadowing through."

There are two types of stitching used for appliqué work: decorative stitching and hidden stitching. Decorative stitching should be consistent and enhance the design. The floss or thread should match, complement or contrast with the fabric while the stitches (of whatever kind) should be properly executed. If hidden stitching is used, it should not be obvious. In this case, the thread color must match the fabric color. The stitches themselves should be small, tight and close together.

All of the above points are important in the execution of good appliqué technique. If only one or two of these are evident on an appliqué quilt, the judge can list them on the comment sheet. But if the comment sheet for an appliqué quilt entry includes the sentence "basic techniques need improvement," you can assume that you have a large number of problems with your appliqué. It's then time to go back to the basics and brush up on all of the elements of the appliqué technique and work at perfecting each of them. You'll then be in better control of appliqué and you, along with the judge who is evaluating your entry in a competition, will find that your basic appliqué technique is acceptable.

WINTER 86
"QUILTING TECHNIQUE NEEDS
IMPROVEMENT"

*When the judges make a
statement on the comment
sheet that "basic techniques
need improvement," it most
likely means that not only
does the top technique
(either piecing, appliqué or
both) need improvement,
but so does the quilting
technique.*

As you know, the three basic techniques of quiltmaking are piecing, appliqué and quilting. When judging quilt competitions, these are the techniques that the judges are evaluating over and over with each quilt. Occasionally, an entry will use some other special technique, but generally speaking, most entries are pieced or appliquéd, or a combination of the two. These two techniques, then, receive careful attention in judging. But above and beyond them, the judges are most frequently evaluating the quilting. Few entries are submitted or accepted in most shows, if they aren't quilted. When the judges make a statement on the comment sheet that "basic techniques need improvement," it most likely means that not only does the top technique (either piecing, appliqué or both) need improvement, but so does the quilting technique. Sometimes, the comment sheet will carry the even more direct statement that "quilting technique needs improvement." Let's look at some of the specifics implied in that statement.

First of all, the quilting stitches should be even, the spaces between them should be even; and the stitches and spaces should be the same length. This is the first detail that bears investigating. The stitches should also be small. But as long as the stitches are not huge, evenness is more important than size. Each of the stitches should also be straight and not cockeyed. The marking tool the maker used to put the quilting design on the work should not be visible. That means: no pencil marks; no residue from washout pens and pencils; and heaven forbid, no ball-point marks.

When the quilting design employs straight lines, either parallel or crossing at some angle, these straight lines should not wave and the spacing between the quilting lines should be even. In other words, the parallel lines should be truly parallel. Where quilting lines cross each other, they should cross smoothly without any puckering at the crossings. By the same token, if the quilting design calls for curved lines, the quilted lines should be smoothly curved. It's important that the startings and endings of the quilting lines should not stick out like sore thumbs; they should be unobtrusive. And, of course, no knots should be visible on the top or on the back of the quilt. The back of the quilt? Yes, the judges do look at the back of the quilt and the quilting on the back. All the quilting stitches should have penetrated all three layers of the quilt without having any gaps in the quilting line on the back. These stitches on the back should also be even.

The tension of the quilting stitches is another factor. The stitches should not be so lazy that they lay loose on the quilt. But, they shouldn't overwork so much that they cause a gathered, puckered or distorted look to the work. These stitches need to have the proper tension, and their size should be appropriate to the fabrics and the batting used in the project. Some fabrics and batting will allow for very fine quilting stitches while other types of fabrics and batting will not accommodate such fine stitching.

All of these factors come into play when a judge is evaluating the quilting on any given entry. So, if you want to avoid a comment that your "basic techniques, especially the quilting, need improvement" consider all of these while you quilt.

SUMMER 89

"HELD UP WELL IN STIFF COMPETITION"

During the process of evaluating a quilt competition, the judges will surely encounter a wide variety of quality among the entries. The design of some of the entered items may range from absolutely smashing to very pedestrian. The same holds true for the workmanship. The execution can be anything from impeccable to "Good grief, it's falling apart!"

When the best is clearly discernible from the worst, judges are able to make their decisions without great difficulty. At the same time, they are able to offer helpful suggestions on comment sheets.

But it is also possible for the judges to be faced with entries which all seem to be of very high caliber. Or, in a large show, once the judges have commented on the lesser entries in a category, they are faced with a thick stack of really good entries from which to choose the award winners. It is in this situation that the decision-making becomes very difficult indeed.

The judges carry on with their usual evaluation methods and choose those entries that are in award contention. It would be nice at this point if the judges had just four quilts left to deal with and the First, Second, Third and Honorable Mention awards could

"Did well against stiff competition." This indicates to the entrant that while the quilt had no major problems and few, if any, minor problems, and was in fact a good quilt, other entries in that same category were even better.

be placed on the appropriate entries. However, quilt judging is rarely that tidy.

What frequently happens is that there are seven or eight award contenders and only four awards. Sometimes this is taken care of by using additional Honorable Mentions. But all competitions are not set up to enable this to be done. If the judges are faced with four awards and seven good quilts – what happens? Well, after a great deal of discussion on each entry and some very difficult decisions, the four awards will be made to the four leading quilts.

But what about those other three good quilts? True. They were good and all the comments on the comment sheets indicate this. It is very hard for an entrant who receives a comment sheet like this to understand why there was no award. Frequently, in this situation, the judges add an additional line to the comment sheet: "Did well against stiff competition." This indicates to the entrant that while the quilt had no major problems and few, if any, minor problems, and was in fact a good quilt, other entries in that same category were even better.

If you should receive a comment sheet at some point that notes your entry "Held up well (or did well) against stiff competition," you will know that the judges considered the entry a very good quilt.

RELATED TOPIC

WINTER 91
SHOULD WE HAVE A JUDGED SHOW?

In addition to being invited to judge competitions, quilt judges are frequently asked by sponsoring groups for advice about planning quilt shows. Sometimes it's a matter of a group gearing up to put on its very first show, whether the group itself is a new one or one long established. Other times it's a group with lots of sponsoring experience. One of the big questions is "Should we have a judged show?" After being asked that question a few times, a quilt judge comes to realize the question is almost always loaded.

The question actually being asked is most likely either "Should we have a judged show? My friends and I think it would be a great idea," or "Should we have a judged show? My friends and I think it would be a stupid idea."

No matter what advice a judge may give, the decision still remains in the hands of the sponsoring group. It is important, though, for the group to be aware of all the possibilities. There are many different kinds of quilt shows being put on by many different groups these days. Some shows are displays of wonderful nostalgic and antique

The bonus with a judged show is that through the comment sheet, the show can educate the quiltmakers and acknowledge their achievements at the same time it educates and entertains the general public.

quilts which it would serve no purpose to judge. Other quilt shows are really course or workshop displays. With this type of show the instructor has already done the evaluating. Still other quilt shows are the results of specific projects or challenges within the group. Undertaken as learning and stretching experiences for the group members, these quilts probably would not need further evaluation.

The general type of show put on by a quilt group is a quite different proposition from the special shows mentioned above. Unfortunately, it can end up with the group being very strongly divided over whether or not their show should be judged. My favorite, seemingly unhelpful, answer to the question "Should we have a judged show?" is "Yes and No." But think about it: there is no problem in having two areas in the same quilt show. One area can be devoted to quilts submitted for judging while the other area can have the quilts entered for display only. In fact, if the group is ambitious and the space adequate, separate areas can be devoted to hanging invitationals, antiques, group workshop projects, bicentennial quilts, garments and all kinds of other special subgroups.

It all comes down to what purpose a group has in sponsoring a quilt show. Most groups put on a show to educate and entertain, and a quilt show limited to displaying quilts will certainly educate and entertain the people who attend the show. The bonus with a judged show is that through the comment sheet, the show can educate the quiltmakers and acknowledge their achievements at the same time it educates and entertains the general public.

If you're a member of a quilt group making these decisions for the first time, or possibly the fifth or tenth time, it's important to keep in mind all of the advantages of each type of show, to consider a show composed of a judged group of entries and a display group, and not to forget the bonuses of a judged show.

May All Your Quilts
Wear Blue Ribbons!

∼American Quilter's Society∼

dedicated to publishing books for today's quilters

The following AQS publications are currently available:

- **Adapting Architectural Details for Quilts,** Carol Wagner, #2282: AQS, 1991, 88 pages, $12.95
- **American Beauties: Rose & Tulip Quilts,** Gwen Marston & Joe Cunningham, #1907: AQS, 1988, 96 pages, $14.95
- **America's Pictorial Quilts,** Caron L. Mosey, #1662: AQS, 1985, 112 pages, hardbound, $19.95
- **Applique Designs: My Mother Taught Me to Sew,** Faye Anderson, #2121: AQS, 1990, 80 pages, $12.95
- **Arkansas Quilts: Arkansas Warmth,** Arkansas Quilter's Guild, Inc., #1908: AQS, 1987, 144 pages, hardbound, $24.95
- **The Art of Hand Applique,** Laura Lee Fritz, #2122: AQS, 1990, 80 pages, $14.95
- **...Ask Helen More About Quilting Designs,** Helen Squire, #2099: AQS, 1990, 54 pages, 17 x 11, spiral-bound, $14.95
- **Award-Winning Quilts & Their Makers: Vol. I, The Best of AQS Shows – 1985-1987,** #2207: AQS, 1991, 232 pages, $24.95
- **Award-Winning Quilts & Their Makers: Vol. II, The Best of AQS Shows – 1988-1989,** #2354: AQS, 1992, 176 pages, $24.95
- **Award-Winning Quilts & Their Makers: Vol. III, The Best of AQS Shows – 1990-1991,** #3425: AQS, 1993, 180 pages, $24.95
- **Classic Basket Quilts,** Elizabeth Porter & Marianne Fons, #2208: AQS, 1991, 128 pages, $16.95
- **A Collection of Favorite Quilts,** Judy Florence, #2119: AQS, 1990, 136 pages, $18.95
- **Creative Machine Art,** Sharee Dawn Roberts, #2355: AQS, 1992, 142 pages, 9 x 9, $24.95
- **Dear Helen, Can You Tell Me?...all about quilting designs,** Helen Squire, #1820: AQS, 1987, 51 pages, 17 x 11, spiral-bound, $12.95
- **Dye Painting!,** Ann Johnston, #3399: AQS, 1992, 88 pages, $19.95
- **Dyeing & Overdyeing of Cotton Fabrics,** Judy Mercer Tescher, #2030: AQS, 1990, 54 pages, $9.95
- **Flavor Quilts for Kids to Make: Complete Instructions for Teaching Children to Dye, Decorate & Sew Quilts,** Jennifer Amor #2356: AQS, 1991, 120 pages, $12.95
- **From Basics to Binding: A Complete Guide to Making Quilts,** Karen Kay Buckley, #2381: AQS, 1992, 160 pages, $16.95
- **Fun & Fancy Machine Quiltmaking,** Lois Smith, #1982: AQS, 1989, 144 pages, $19.95
- **Gallery of American Quilts 1830-1991: Book III,** #3421: AQS, 1992, 128 pages, $19.95
- **The Grand Finale: A Quilter's Guide to Finishing Projects,** Linda Denner, #1924: AQS, 1988, 96 pages, $14.95
- **Heirloom Miniatures,** Tina M. Gravatt, #2097: AQS, 1990, 64 pages, $9.95
- **Infinite Stars,** Gayle Bong, #2283: AQS, 1992, 72 pages, $12.95
- **The Ins and Outs: Perfecting the Quilting Stitch,** Patricia J. Morris, #2120: AQS, 1990, 96 pages, $9.95
- **Irish Chain Quilts: A Workbook of Irish Chains & Related Patterns,** Joyce B. Peaden, #1906: AQS, 1988, 96 pages, $14.95
- **The Log Cabin Returns to Kentucky: Quilts from the Pilgrim/Roy Collection,** Gerald Roy and Paul Pilgrim, #3329: AQS, 1992, 36 pages, 9 x 7, $12.95
- **Marbling Fabrics for Quilts: A Guide for Learning & Teaching,** Kathy Fawcett & Carol Shoaf, #2206: AQS, 1991, 72 pages, softbound, $12.95
- **More Projects and Patterns: A Second Collection of Favorite Quilts,** Judy Florence, #3330: AQS, 1992, 152 pages, $18.95
- **Nancy Crow: Quilts and Influences,** Nancy Crow, #1981: AQS, 1990, 256 pages, 9 x 12, hardcover, $29.95
- **Nancy Crow: Work in Transition,** Nancy Crow, #3331: AQS, 1992, 32 pages, 9 x 10, $12.95
- **New Jersey Quilts – 1777 to 1950: Contributions to an American Tradition,** The Heritage Quilt Project of New Jersey; text by Rachel Cochran, Rita Erickson, Natalie Hart & Barbara Schaffer, #3332: AQS, 1992, 256 pages, $29.95
- **No Dragons on My Quilt,** Jean Ray Laury with Ritva Laury & Lizabeth Laury, #2153: AQS, 1990, 52 pages, hardcover, $12.95
- **Oklahoma Heritage Quilts,** Oklahoma Quilt Heritage Project #2032: AQS, 1990, 144 pages, $19.95
- **Old Favorites in Miniature,** Tina M. Gravatt, #3469: AQS, 1993, 104 pages, $15.95.
- **Quilt Groups Today: Who They Are, Where They Meet, What They Do, and How to Contact Them; A Complete Guide for 1992-1993,** #3308: AQS, 1992, 336 pages, $14.95
- **Quilting Patterns from Native American Designs,** Dr. Joyce Mori, #3467: AQS, 1993, 80 pages, $12.95
- **Quilting with Style: Principles for Great Pattern Design,** Gwen Marston & Joe Cunningham, #3470: AQS, 1993, 192 pages, 9" x 12", hardcover, $24.95.
- **Quiltmaker's Guide: Basics & Beyond,** Carol Doak, #2284: AQS, 1992, 208 pages, $19.95
- **Quilts: Old & New, A Similar View,** Paul D. Pilgrim and Gerald E. Roy, #3715: AQS, 1993, 40 pages, $12.95
- **Quilts: The Permanent Collection – MAQS,** #2257: AQS, 1991, 100 pages, 10 x 6½, $9.95
- **Sensational Scrap Quilts,** Darra Duffy Williamson, #2357: AQS, 1992, 152 pages, $24.95
- **Show Me Helen...How to Use Quilting Designs,** Helen Squire, #3375: AQS, 1993, 155 pages, $15.95
- **Sets & Borders,** Gwen Marston & Joe Cunningham, #1821: AQS, 1987, 104 pages, $14.95
- **Somewhere in Between: Quilts and Quilters of Illinois,** Rita Barrow Barber, #1790: AQS, 1986, 78 pages, $14.95
- **Stenciled Quilts for Christmas,** Marie Monteith Sturmer, #2098: AQS, 1990, 104 pages, $14.95
- **A Treasury of Quilting Designs,** Linda Goodmon Emery, #2029: AQS, 1990, 80 pages, 14 x 11, spiral-bound, $14.95
- **Wonderful Wearables: A Celebration of Creative Clothing,** Virginia Avery, #2286: AQS, 1991, 184 pages, $24.95

These books can be found in local bookstores and quilt shops. If you are unable to locate a title in your area, you can order by mail from AQS, P.O. Box 3290, Paducah, KY 42002-3290.
Please add $1 for the first book and 40¢ for each additional one to cover postage and handling.
(International orders please add $1.50 for the first book and $1 for each additional one.)